For Rulers

FOR RULERS

PRIMING POLITICAL LEADERS FOR SAVING HUMANITY FROM ITSELF

YEHEZKEL DROR

The Hebrew University of Jerusalem

Westphalia Press

An Imprint of the Policy Studies Organization

Washington, DC

2017

For Rulers
All Rights Reserved © 2017 by Policy Studies Organization

Westphalia Press
An imprint of Policy Studies Organization
1527 New Hampshire Ave., NW
Washington, D.C. 20036
info@ipsonet.org

ISBN-10: 1-63391-552-2
ISBN-13: 978-1-63391-552-7

Library of Congress Control Number: 2017911733
Westphalia Press, Washington, DC

Cover and interior design by Jeffrey Barnes
jbarnesbook.design

Daniel Gutierrez-Sandoval, Executive Director
PSO and Westphalia Press

Updated material and comments on this edition
can be found at the Westphalia Press website:
www.westphaliapress.org

MAIN BOOKS BY YEHEZKEL DROR

Public Policymaking Reexamined

Crazy States: A Counterconventional Strategic Problem

Design for Policy Sciences

Ventures in Policy Sciences: Concepts and Applications

Policymaking Under Adversity

The Capacity to Govern: A Report to the Club of Rome

Israeli Statecraft: National Security Challenges and Responses

Avant-Garde Politician: Leaders for a New Epoch

For My RAND Corporation Friends
Deceased or Still Kicking,
Advising Rulers
However Often in Vain.
Thanks for All I Learned
While Agitating You with "Crazy" Ideas

CONTENTS

1. Preamble

1.1 This is an urgent Memo trying to convince you to remake yourself into a critically novel type of political leader qualified to serve as a *Homo Sapiens* Governor (in short HSG, plural HSGs) participating in the Promethean mission of saving humanity from itself.

1.2 I hurried to write this Memo because its message is immediately needed. This is so thanks to the accelerating speed at which the human species is cascading through a phase transformation into a radically novel epoch in which it can reshape vital aspects of Earth, change main features of human beings, perhaps procreate a superior human-oid species and even super-intelligent "machines," but also can quite easily terminate its own existence.

1.3 The cascading power supplied by science and technology to humanity is bipolar: it enables unprecedented human thriving or dev-astating catastrophes, up to endangering modern civilization and, to reemphasize a fatal danger, even ending the existence of the human species.

1.4 Thus, in orders of magnitudes, however callous this may seem, killing and maiming more than, say, between 50 and 100 million humans is a global catastrophe. The maintainability of civilization is endangered if more than half of humanity, mainly in the centers of global civilization, are killed. Survival of less than at least three concentrations of a couple of hundred healthy humans endangers the continuing existence of the species.

1.5 Unavoidably, political leaders will fulfill a critical role in shaping the uses and misuses of the power to shape human futures. But contemporary types of senior politicians are glaringly underqualified for coping with emerging fateful challenges. Please read the summary of the 2016 *Report of the UK Committee of Privy Counsellors on the Iraq War*. Or, to stay with the UK, which has a relatively good though increasingly outdated governance machinery, read the House of Commons, Foreign Affairs Committee 2016 document *Libya: Examination of intervention and collapse and the UK's future policy options*. They show beyond any shadow of doubt that even intelligent prime ministers assisted by highly professional staffs are unable to cope well with complex "normal" issues. A fortiori, they cannot be relied upon to handle adequately the fateful quagmires sure to increasingly challenge humanity. Therefore, a much improved genre of political leaders is urgently needed. Without it survival and thriving requirements cannot be met and the long-term existence of the human species is seriously endangered.

1.6 This Memo is submitted to help you overcome the quality deficit of contemporary political leaders by becoming an HSG. It is written for rulers, however formally titled, as well as rulership-aspirants and for all who exert major influence on rulers, such as senior advisors.

1.7 Not less important addressees are persons who should become rulers but are not eager to do so. Politics as now constituted does not attract and admit the best of the best, such as outstanding scientists, top quality policy scholars, and innovative philosophers. If you are one of them, I hope this Memo may encourage you to overcome your nausea from the smell of "politics as usual," strive to become a senior politician, and transform politics into a noble vocation capable of fulfilling its increasingly fateful tasks.

1.8 This text also aims at outstanding students from whom a new genre of prime political leaders should sprout. And, last but far from least, there is no hope for the emergence of the required novel rulers and fulfillment of their mission without the cooperation of other future-impactors and broad public support. Therefore, this Memo is also relevant for entrepreneurs, philanthropists, mass-media moguls, and indeed all who are worried about the future of humanity and realize that "politics as usual" is unable to take care of it.

1.9 Moving in the directions suggested in the Memo also requires many innovations in leadership studies and mentoring, as well as in policy studies and public policy teaching. Researchers, teachers, practitioners, and learners in these domains may find it quite relevant.

1.10 The Memo starts with presenting the new epoch into which humanity is cascading and the fateful choices it poses to the human species and to HSGs as a new genre of political leaders qualified to try and save humanity from itself. Next some main humanity-craft principles are presented, leading to a mapping of core qualities needed by your mind for fulfilling your Promethean mission. Finally, your existential choice to try and become a qualified HSG is posed.

1.11 To help you go deeper into the main subject, a recommended reading list is provided. But take care to get the most recent editions and look for up-to-date texts fitting your interests.

2. Promethean Mission

2.1 The emerging leap in human power, supplied by science and technology, can enable unimaginable pluralistic thriving and perhaps steps toward the stars. But it also poses serious and even fatal risks to the human species. Never before has humankind faced such fateful choices how to use its power.

2.2 Even if you are an outstanding "ordinary" ruler making important decisions, up to choosing war or peace, nothing in your experience and studies prepared you for the monumental issues increasingly facing the human species. Humanity as a whole is not prepared for them and largely unaware of their emergence. Therefore, my suggestion to you to try and become an HSG offers an exhilarating, historic-making, but extremely demanding undertaking raising you at least somewhat to the level of what Hegel called a "world-historic figure," even if on a small scale and not widely recognized as such.

2.3 Doing your best to cope with the fateful choices increasingly facing humanity is a Promethean mission: in the dictionary sense of "daring, creative, original," and in the Greek mythological sense of helping humanity. Lord Byron put it well in his 1816 poem *Prometheus*:

> "To render with thy precepts less
>
> The sum of human wretchedness,
>
> And strengthen Man with his own mind"

2.4 The time horizon recommended for pondering your mission is a "now-time" of 5–10 years, an outlook and lead time of 50–100 years, and some speculations on an undefined further-off future. These time horizons are, respectively, short enough for well-based action and long enough for anchoring your choices in accelerating deep evolutionary processes.

2.5 Given the lengthening life expectancy of the better-off parts of humanity, to which you most likely belong, 100 years is in subjective time much shorter now than in the past, and will become even shorter during your life. But history is accelerating, with more events and process changes taking place in shorter time spans. Therefore, a main time horizon of 50–100 years is both essential and reasonable for your concerns.

2.6 The metaphysical assumption which I recommend for your mission is this-worldly. Humanity exists on the edge of the unknowable. It is up to you to decide what transcendental beliefs, if any, to accept as "true". But, with one critical exception, they should not shape your mission. The exception concerns meta-ethics, which constitutes the normative basis for the values which should guide you in fulfilling your mission, as discussed in Section 7 of this Memo.

3. ANTHROPOREGENESIS

3.1 "Anthropocene" is a recently coined term for the epoch in which many geologically important features of the Earth are significantly influenced by human activities. In most views it started with the Industrial Revolution in the second half of the eighteenth and the first half of the nineteenth century. But the mid-twentieth century is a much more fateful date for *Homo sapiens*. The production and use of atomic bombs in 1945 starting a new epoch, which I call "Anthroporegenesis"—in which humanity has not only the power to transform features of Earth critical for humanity, but also to recreate main properties of human beings, with or without some kind of super-species taking over, and also kill the human sapiens species.

3.2 Surging science and technology will enable humans to live longer and better, upgrade mental abilities, and construct super-tech "Gardens of Eden" to serve as habitats for humans. Human cloning, creation of other intelligent entities cohabiting with humanity, and perhaps human settlements beyond Earth may also become feasible. But, as stated by one of the creators of nuclear bombs, "the scientific method does not filter for benevolence". The surging power supplied to humanity by science and technology can cause serious disruptions, catastrophes, bring about the destruction of modern civilization, and—quite easily and even likely in some views—also eradicate the human species.

3.3 It is not science and technology which endangers humanity, but human choices or errors. Please keep this crucial understanding in mind when taking a look at possible human-caused extinction of the human species, prevention of which is your overriding first duty:

- Synthesis in a kitchen laboratory and diffusion of an air-carried lethal virus immune to all antidotes by a doomsday sect wishing to rid Gaia of humanity.

- Production of "super-intelligent" robots who take over the world and eliminate humanity.

- A high-power physical experiment causes an Earth-destructing chain reaction.

- Nanorobots get out of control and kill all humans.

- The impact of a large body from space, which could have been prevented by timely countermeasures, kills most of life on Earth including all humans.

- Far from unlikely, a nuclear war making Earth uninhabitable for humans.

3.4 Your duty is also to prevent human-caused catastrophes and mass suffering, even if they do not endanger the survival of the human species. These include milder versions of the terminal contingencies above with additions, such as:

- Scarcity of essential materials, which is quite likely if world population reaches 11 billion in 2100, as predicted by a 2015 United Nations projection.

- Molecular engineering which may provide substitutes for resources, but carries dangers of its own: thus, if it becomes possible to realize the dream of Alchemy and mutate materials, such as transforming coal into high-grade large diamonds undistinguishable from natural ones (remember, both are different forms of carbon), or in transforming a cheap element into gold, socio-economy havoc is sure to follow.

- Large-scale unemployment due to advanced robots taking over many white collar jobs, while potentially a blessing if well handled, causes disruptive and also bloody social turmoil.

- Humanity-caused climate changes causing catastrophic conflicts, epidemics, and scarcities killing more than 10% of humanity.

3.5 A complex set of explosive issues is posed by human enhancement, which may add intolerable biological inequality to socio-economic ones. Thus the very likely "soft enhancement" possibility to prolong life expectancy to, say, 150 high-quality years, but at a cost of two million dollars, will produce a degree of inequality which no society will be able to tolerate, easily leading to large-scale revolutionary violence—all the more as studies of history indicate that it is nearly impossible to reduce extreme inequality peacefully.

3.6 Very worrying while also being very promising are "hard" human enhancements leading to "post-humanity", human cloning, "eternal life" etc. In addition to socio-economic breakdowns, such possibilities impact on main religions and raise unprecedented and very divisive questions on the meaning of human existence. These easily result in large-scale conflicts producing at least much "Hell on Earth," and perhaps civilizational decline.

3.7 Emerging human power can also result in multiple human thriving; and, if so decided, advancement toward "Homo superior." But avoiding terminal and catastrophic risks is the prime imperative at the core of your Promethean mission as an HSG, combined with facilitating uses for the better.

3.8 To sum up: **the emerging epoch of Anthroporegenesis is characterized by surging human power to reshape Earth, remake the human species, and perhaps procreate Homo superior and super-intelligent non-human entities. These and other uses of increasing human regenesis power can result in catastrophes and also endanger the existence of the human species. But they can also enable unimaginable pluralistic human thriving. Reducing the risks, with absolute priority to prevent species self-destruction, while facilitating novel forms of thriving—these constitute your Promethean mission as an HSG.**

3.9 Please note that most of what is presented in this section, and in this Memo as a whole, is far from the minds of the vast majority of humanity, including nearly all political leaders. Yet, as an HSG, you must know that what seems impossible, or is unthinkable by most humans, can happen; and much of it is very likely to happen in the foreseeable future. You have to anticipate it, ponder on it, and prepare for it!

4. HUMAN EVOLUTION AT STAKE

4.1 The Anthroporegenesis epoch raises a range of philosophic questions on evolutionary processes: are they deterministically leading to the emergence of more complex sentient beings, with *Homo sapiens* being displaced by a Homo superior species or even spiritual machines, paradoxically procreated by humanity at the cost of its own existence? Is the leap in human power mainly a result of random effects? Are the Anthroporegenesis processes mainly shaped by inherent dynamics or by human choices? Is humanity evolving toward a more or less stable "end of history," for instance with a spiritual civilization taking over? Will there be repetitive cycles of humanity destroying its socio-technological civilization and then rebuilding it? Or is something inconceivable by the human mind likely to come?

4.2 Such and additional alternative futures are possible, but probably none is predetermined. Instead, the deep and fateful feature of the epoch of Anthroporegenesis is the revolutionary transformation of the significance of human decisions from marginal impacts on the future of the human species to increasingly shaping it. Even if we cannot be sure that this is true, from a non-fatalistic standpoint this is recommended as the "as-if" working assumption leading to maximal human efforts to impact on the future for the better, even if we know that this may be in vain. In such efforts, HSGs fulfill a critical role, which is at the center of this Memo.

4.3 It is very likely that human evolution has led *Homo sapiens* into a trap, which we may be unable to exit. This trap provides humanity with the power to significantly shape its future as a species, but without the wisdom needed to do so well—making self-elimination quite likely, and major human-caused catastrophes nearly certain.

4.4 Contrary views are widely accepted, often also by political leaders who should know better, on an assured good future for humanity, even if the way to it is not smooth and also bloody. Such views rely on the "cunning" of history, innate goodness of human beings, guaranteed global adoption of democratic free market liberalism, and so on. Yet, these are not only figments of the imagination, but contradict the lessons of history, evolution-imprinted propensities of humans, and contemporary processes. You as an HSG must free your mind from such illusions, trust in a "right side of history," and similar *fata morgana*. Instead, you have to toil and trouble to swerve human history from what is a very dangerous direction into a desirable one, knowing that success is not assured but doing your very best.

4.5 A short science fiction story by Frederic Brown called "The Weapon" puts the issue squarely: a sudden visitor to a famous scientist tries to convince him to stop developing an ultimate weapon because it endangers humanity, but fails. The scientist goes to the kitchen to bring the guest some water. When returning the guest is gone, but the retarded child of the scientist has in his hand a gift from the visitor: a loaded revolver. The shocked scientist takes the revolved from his son thinking "only a madman would give a loaded revolver to an idiot".

4.6 Is humanity "an idiot?" The answer I propose is "often, but not completely so." But if you ask if most political leaders are idiots, my answer is "they surely are not idiots. But the vast majority of them lack the values, perspectives, understandings, pondering abilities and other qualities of the mind which are increasingly essential for coping with the evolutionary trap in which humanity is ensnared."

4.7 On the basis of historic and comparative studies and quite some personal experience of working with rulers in a variety of countries, I fully agree with the succinct assessment by David Rothkopf (in *The Great Questions of Tomorrow*, 2017, pp. 9 and 51-52): "many of those in position of power and their supporters are so actively trying to cling to the past we can almost hear their fingernails clawing at the earth as they try to avoid accepting the inevitable and momentous changes to come" and "They aren't asking the right questions. Typically, they don't even know what the questions are."

4.8 This assessment, which I think is fully supported by hard facts, is very worrying. It is doubtful that humanity and its contemporary type of political leaders are able to cope with the awesome power provided by leaping science and technology. On the contrary, all we know on human individual and collective propensities as well political leadership is a cause for extreme worry. Therefore, for humanity to thrive, and at least survive so as to have a chance to do better in the future, the quality of its leaders, including first of all political leaders, must change radically for the better, by becoming much more of what I call Homo sapiens governors.

4.9 The most fateful part of your mission is assuring as far as possible species survival. Human happiness, justice, artistic achievements, material wellbeing etc. are important, but come second and third after assuring the survival of humanity. A future generation may somehow decide to procreate a superior species at the cost of the existence of Homo sapiens, but this possibility is far beyond you longest time horizon. You can safely leave it for speculations and counter-factual thought experiments by philosophers and theologians.

4.10 Contrary to what should receive top priority, namely assuring humanity has a future, most of the serious dangers are not at the center of public and political agendas. The dangers of global nuclear war receive some thought, as illustrated by the Doomsday Clock of the *Bulletin of the Nuclear Scientists*. Quite some attention, though little action, is given to climate change. Obsolete ideas on coping with conventional terrorism are widely discussed. But the most fatal dangers are hardly taken up in public discourse nor included in political agenda. For sure, they are not effectively confronted.

4.11 This dangerous neglect is fully reflected, for instance, in the Sustainable Development Goals in force since 2016. These goals are important and honorable, trying to advance human thriving. But they are very wrong in not putting survival of the human species at the center, taking it implicitly and mistakenly as granted.

4.12 Altogether, tribal concerns, in a broad meaning of that term, continue to dominate attention, feelings, thinking, and efforts. This is conceptually expressed in pronouncements by rulers, such as "my country comes first", as well as public choices, such as Brexit. Demonstrating deep tribalism is the very term "international organizations," instead of "global governance". The prevailing politics of climate change fully illustrates the feebleness of *raison d'humanité* when compared with what are narrowly regarded as "national interests."

4.13 All this should have been obvious and efforts should have been made to change it when, for the first time in the history of Earth, a human-produced self-sustained reaction in an uranium pile went critical, on December 2, 1942 at 1553 Chicago time, which was the beginning of a new world. Leo Szilard, the one scientist probably most responsible for the achievement, thought this day will go down as a black day in the history of mankind. Even the half-blind should have realized that humanity moved through a threshold when the bright glare of "trinity," the explosion of the first nuclear bomb ever, reached their eyes on July 16, 1945, 5:29 am 45 seconds.

4.14 Some of the scientists who made nuclear fission and nuclear bombs possible were aware of their danger to the survival of humanity (as were a few political leaders, but without drawing practical conclusions). As formulated later by Niels Bohr, a physicist second only to Albert Einstein, "the very necessity of a concerted effort to forestall … ominous threats to civilization would offer quite unique opportunities to bridge international divergences." But he was far too optimistic: it takes much more to teach political leaders, and humanity as a whole, to change their ways.

4.15 Senior scientists involved in the development of the nuclear bomb submitted some prudent proposals to top level USA decision makers. But these, as should be expected by all but politics-naïve scientists and reality-distant dreamers, gave priority to short-term aims, including domestic political ones. I cannot imagine a stronger proof of the incapability of the contemporary type of political leaders to assure the long-term existence and thriving of the human species than their mishandling of the dangers posed by nuclear weapons, including the misconceived "Atoms for Peace" policy, which enabled proliferation.

4.16 What has been called the "Republic of Science" also is guilty of dereliction of duty. As for now, science and technology continue at accelerating speed to provide humanity with additional very dangerous power, such as technologies for mutating viruses in kitchen laboratories, without insisting on adequate global control of its uses. Francis Bacon, when proclaiming "knowledge is power," was less reckless. He stated in his utopia *The New Atlantis* (1627):

> "... we have consultations, which of the inventions and experiences which we have discovered shall be published, and which not: and take all an oath of secrecy, for the concealing of those which we think fit to keep secret: though some of those we do reveal sometimes to the state and some not."

4.17 Given their fateful role and knowledge, select scientists should have an authoritative say in decisions on the production and uses of dangerous knowledge, including some becoming HSGs. But more is required from scientists, locally and globally, as part of progressing toward quality politics and global governance, to be discussed in Sections 20 and 21.

5. Existential Human Species Choices

5.1 The core idea of existential philosophy is that a person always has some scope for choosing what to do, is responsible for his choices and has to be willing to bear their consequences. Applied to humanity as a species, up to the Anthroporegenesis its freedom of action was limited and did not include choosing between alternative long-term species futures, as distinct from local shorter-term ones. But this situation is changing totally, with humankind having a choice between many al-

FOR RULERS

ternative collective futures, if—and this is a critical "if"—it is able to deliberate and implement choices, either directly or—and this is the only realistic option in the foreseeable future—via agents acting on behalf of and for humankind, though largely self-selected.

5.2 Two hypothetical possibilities illustrate the modalities of the human species acting as a deliberative and effective actor: (1) main choices are made by all adult persons on Earth, either by some kind of representative democracy, or/and by global referenda; (2) A global ruler or authoritarian global government acts as a kind of "Global Leviathan," in line with the concept proposed by Thomas Hobbes but attenuated, making choices shaping the future of the human species and enforcing them worldwide, without taking into account the wishes of the billions of presently living humans.

5.3 The vast majority of humans lacks the knowledge to pass judgment on very complex moral-technical choices as posed to humanity in the Anthroporegenesis epoch; and a Global Leviathan, even if effectively curbed, is dangerous and impossible to set up under ordinary conditions. However, if a number of serious catastrophes produce a major global crisis, some approximation of decisive global governance based on a few major powers may become both necessary and feasible.

5.4 Much preferable is development of a global guidance cluster of social leaders, outstanding entrepreneurs, select scientists and technology developers, spiritual-philosophic thinkers, a sprinkling of artists, together with HSGs at its core. It would try to crystallize agreement on main critical issues facing humanity and mobilize broad support for appropriate action by a novel global governance system.

5.5 In the longer run, adequate coping with fateful choices requires

15

strengthening humanity as a collective actor on the basis of a shared "we" feeling. However, this too may have to wait till catastrophes teach humanity that tribalism will lead to disasters and all of humanity is in "one increasingly leaky boat."

5.6 All future-impacting choices are made by presently living humans, without future generations having a say. Therefore, even the most democratic future-shaping choices by humans living at any time cannot be really "participatory." This is an unavoidable result of the arrow of time. No effort by contemporary humans to try and guess what future generations may wish, beyond basics such as "existing" (which too may not fit the values of some future generations), is no more than a wild speculation. It follows, that logically there cannot exist "democratic choices" impacting on future generations, if democracy is understood, as it usually is, giving to all who have to bear the consequences of choices a chance to influence them.

5.7 It follows that when you as an HSG make choices which you have good reasons to regard as having significant impact on the next and even later generations, the question if you represent or at least reflect contemporary humanity becomes at least partly irrelevant. This is very important for the issue of your legitimacy in making choices impacting on future generations, to which I shall return toward the end of the Memo.

5.8 This finding on lacking the agreement of future generations to choices made now which will impact on them, requires ethically from HSGs, and indeed all political leaders and also other future-impactors, a maximal efforts to make the best possible decisions based on outstanding moral and intellectual virtues and a determined effort to ponder and act optimally in terms of the longer-range evolution of the human species. (Please note, throughout this Memo I use the broader term "pondering" instead of "thinking." Pondering includes both conscious thinking and subconscious mental processes, such as intuition, creativity, inspiration, imagination, and more).

6. *HOMO SAPIENS* GOVERNORS TO THE FORE

6.1 Political leaders often make potent decisions. But, given the realities of globalization and the Internet, heads of large global enterprises, path-breaking scientists and technologists, a few "celebrities," and social-cultural leaders often exert more influence. Thus, both the sexual and the Internet revolutions and much of the scientific and technological epoch-transformation have politicians running after them. Similarly, terrorism and other forms of violence are shaping politics, the dictum of Clausewitz about war as a continuation of politics/policy being increasingly incorrect. Instead politics is trying to catch up with various forms of "war," such as escalating cyber-attacks, without success.

6.2 Paradigm-changing thinkers, such as Marx and Freud, transformed the world more than any political leader; and a few books, such as *Uncle Tom's Cabin* by Harriet Beecher Stowe and *Silent Spring* by Rachel Carlson, had more profound impact on public values and "great politics" than any politician—not to speak about Martin Luther and the Protestant Reformation. Luckily, subject to essential constraints against humanity-endangering contents, this is sure to continue, otherwise cultures will be paralyzed and liberty may vanish from the Earth.

6.3 However, the fateful choices faced by humanity in the Anthroporegenesis epoch on the uses and mis-uses of Earth and humanity-

remaking power are of a much higher order of deliberate intervention with the future evolution of the human species, being in part of
fatal significance. Therefore they are beyond the legitimate authority
of markets, scientists and technologists, free-floating thinkers, social
movements, preachers, and so on. And leaving them to the drift of
non-steered historical processes is a sure way to disasters.

6.4 A variety of actors will and should continue to fulfill important
roles in the unfolding of humanity, some of them, such as scientists,
even more so than in the past. But fateful choices have to be made by
political leaders, or at least be endorsed and accepted by them. This requirement makes politics in some crucial respects the most important
of all human-species-level social institutions, processes and vocations,
with upgrading of the quality of politics, and in particular key political
leaders, becoming a top priority.

6.5 Three lines of reasoning support this conclusion: (1) "politicians"
are by definition entitled to make decisions on behalf of and for societies in which they are elected or otherwise selected or legitimized;
(2) religious and other spiritual leaders may be accepted as the highest
decision makers by their followers, but only the strata of politicians is
explicitly or implicitly in charge of major decisions shaping the future
of societies and of humanity as a whole; (3) with minor exceptions,
politicians have a monopoly on legislation and on activating massive
instruments of violence as may be necessary.

6.6 To further clarify the matter, let us take up the proposal of Plato
in his dialogue *The Republic* that philosophers should serve as rulers.
With all its merits and its importance for the idea of HSGs, it suffers
from an internal contradiction: serving as rulers would ipso facto make
the philosophers into "politicians," though selected according to merit

instead elections, party caucus, inheritance, and so on.

6.7 If all major decisions are made by referenda or small group agreement, or collective choice is abolished in favor of some form of anarchism, then "politics" as practiced by humanity since living in large groups is eliminated. Something like this can happen if humanity is thrown back to hunting, gathering, and primitive agriculture by small groups; or if in a "paradisiac" future humanity lives in relatively autarkic small self-governing super-high-tech cities. But, leaving aside such hypothetical futures, the following conclusion is unavoidable, however disturbing: **In the Anthroporegenesis epoch politicians, however constrained, should be in charge, formally and in fact, of major collective choices, including fateful decisions on the future of the human species "to be, not to be, what to be."**

6.8 Dependence on political leaders for fateful choices is not a cause for celebration. The record of most of them during known human history demonstrates a preponderance of dismal behavior and avoidable major errors, with the outbreak of the First World War being a paradigmatic example.

6.9 Most contemporary political leaders are clearly unable to cope with crucial global issues, including relatively clear ones, such as climate change. They focus on current issues, often discounting the future; are beholden to tribal loyalties; lack understanding of the issues posed by surging science and technology; are unable to reconsider clearly dysfunctional values and goals, and so on. Also, far too many are morally corrupt, giving more weight to staying in power and often also to enriching themselves and their families than coping with important issues.

6.10 But all is not lost. Many inadequacies of political leaders are caused by the constraints imposed on them, such as coalition governments, exaggerated judicial interventions, dependence on capital and various interest groups, mass media pressures, populistic psychology, proliferating social networks, global processes beyond control by any political leader in the absence of effective global governance, and more. Such chains can be loosened by constitutional reforms, but these usually become feasible only when crises shatter the hold of the past on the future.

6.11 Very significantly, the existence of quite a number of outstanding recent or still active political and intellectual leaders, though by far all too few, proves that required qualities are not utopian. Given fitting positions and adequate authority, personalities such as the following could probably cope well with the fateful issues facing humanity: Konrad Adenauer, Ehud Barak, Niels Bohr, Deng Xiaoping, Ricardo Díez-Hochleitner, Bill Gates, Mikhail Gorbachev, Al Gore, Dag Hammarskjold, Henry Kissinger, Vladimir Lenin, Nelson Mandela, Angela Merkel, Jean Monnet, Alva and Gunnar Myrdal, Jawaharlal Nehru, Barack Obama, Leo Szilard, Justin Trudeau, and Lee Kuan Yew.

6.12 Such examples demonstrate that being an HSG is not beyond human capacities, though we cannot be sure that even the best possible "ruler of humanity" can prevent the self-destruction of the species. And, however optimal choices by HSGs may be, a lot of blood and pain on humanity's way through the Anthroporegenesis is unavoidable—and may in fact be essential for bringing about the necessary changes in human desires, behavior, values, institutions, and leadership.

6.13 But do not fool yourself: the "self-help" literature promising that everyone can be an outstanding leader is bullshit. It is very likely that only a miniscule part of humanity has the intrinsic potential to become HSGs making adequate choices of fateful potent for the future of the human species. However, there are such persons, however much they must toil to develop essential qualities and get a chance to realize their potential.

6.14 Specification of the qualities required from HSGs must wait till the substance of their Promethean mission is presented in the form of humanity-craft principles (in the sense of statecraft principles, but applying to humankind as a whole), from which required core qualities of their minds can be derived. But to leave the idea of HSGs empty no longer, some postulates can be preliminarily presented now, to be elaborated and justified throughout the following parts of the Memo:

Postulate One: In order to save humanity from itself a growing number of HSGs is indispensable. But all public leaders and also private powerholders are morally obliged to take into account in their choices the requirement of long-term existence and thriving of the Homo sapiens species.

Postulate Two: In order to fulfill their Promethean mission of saving humanity from itself by developing and enforcing "humanity-craft," HSGs need a plenitude of command clout. This is all the more essential as the radical innovativeness of much of humanity-craft will unavoidably trigger strenuous opposition and generate stubborn resistance (e.g., accusing Pope Francis of spreading heresy).

Postulate Three: Given that HSGs too are neither Platonic rulers nor Confucian saints, carefully calibrated checks and balances are essential.

Postulate Four: With the partial exception of global governance bodies, political leaders, including HSGs, are formally legitimated as caretakers of the interests of their polity—not for taking care of the future of humanity. Therefore, HSGs often have no alternative other than "self-legitimation," on the moral bases of "dire humankind necessity."

<u>Postulate Five</u>: Outstanding and scarce personal, moral and intellectual virtues, as well as leadership qualities, are essential for being an HSG, justifiable self-anointment as HSGs, and wide acceptance as such.

<u>Postulate Six</u>: Formal governance status can provide much of the authority needed by HSGs. Carefully crafted presidential regimes do so often better than multi-party parliamentary-cabinet regimes, with unstable coalitions being the worst of all.

<u>Postulate Seven</u>: Constitutions, a variety of legal instruments, and courts should grant HSGs the discretion and authority they need, while guarding against unessential interventions with personal and group rights. Meeting this essential requirement requires quite some constitution rewriting, court reforms, and innovative legislation.

<u>Postulate Eight</u>: Without a radically novel global order which includes decisive global governance institutions, even a plenitude of fully qualified HSGs will not be able to fulfill its mission and save humanity from itself.

<u>Conclusion</u>: Decisive political leaders with HSG qualities are essential for saving humanity from itself. To fulfill adequately their Promethean mission, they need, in addition to very demanding personal, moral and intellectual virtues, much authority, a selectively commanding

global governance base, and growing global public support—all subject to adequate safeguards.

7. Basic Norm: *Homo Sapiens* Future is the Measure of all Things

7.1 Your nature as an HSG and the humanity-craft you compose/approve and implement are, as all policies and major decisions but even more so, embedded in a basic norm. The classical Greek philosopher Protagoras is reputed to have said "man is the measure of all things." I reformulate it and propose the following basic norm for HSGs and all of humanity-craft: *Homo sapiens* future is the measure of all things, reformulated somewhat more operationally as ***Homo sapiens* long-term thriving, and, first of all, the survival of the human species, is the measure of all things.**

7.2 Depending on your religious and other basic beliefs, which serve as your personal metaethics, you may like to add some elements to the basic norm, such as "the Ten Commandments", "avoiding causing pain to other intelligent animals," and "basic human rights." But my advice is not to dilute the proposed basic norm by many additions, and definitely not to add elements which conflict with it.

7.3 The proposed basic norm shifts emphasis to the human species as a collection and increasingly a collective of self-conscious human beings, as opposed to contemporary emphasis on humans as individual persons. For most purposes this makes no substantive difference, because "humanity" includes all humans in the past, now and in the future, without any organismic connotation. Also, "humans" and "humanity" are "complementary," in the sense of quantum theory where the term refers to unlike features of what is one and the same phenomenon (such as the dual nature of light as both a particle and a wave).

7.4 However, there are many cases of conflict, such as between standards of living of humans as individuals now and conserving essential resources for the long-term existence of the human species. Or, to take a more painful tragic dilemma, for assuring the future of the human species it may be necessary to prohibit some types of biological research which can help a number of individuals suffering from an otherwise incurable and painful disease, but which enables doomsday fanatics to synthesize viruses killing large parts of humanity.

7.5 Given conflicts between human desires and needs and assuring the long-term existence of the human species, the proposed basic norm requires from you as an HSG to give priority to the latter. But be aware that it may be very difficult emotionally and politically to give priority to an abstract future of humankind over the wellbeing of concrete persons here and now.

7.6 There is a deeper problem, namely what kind of "survival" is morally worth assuring. Thus, assuming as a thought experiment that the only way to assure the long-term survival of the human species is a repressive global dictatorship in which most humans are miserable while a small elite thrives—is such a future worth saving? Given such considerations, it might be better to reformulate the basic norm by adding "worthy" to survival, so that it postulates "*Homo sapiens* long-term thriving, and above all the *worthy* survival of the human species, are the measure of all things." But this begs the question what will humans in the future regard as "worthy." Also a period of "unworthy" survival may be tolerable because it may give way to "worthy" survival.

Therefore, I trend to stick to the formulae *Homo sapiens* long-term thriving, and, first of all, the survival of the human species is the measure of all things.

7.7 There is one already mentioned possible exception to the proposed basic norm, namely if and when humanity should decide to prefer procreation of a superior species (including "spiritual machines") to its own existence. But this "to be or create a new species" choice is for future generations to decide, with present actions which may limit future options to be avoided unless essential for species survival.

7.8 This is the place to deconstruct some fashionable terms which are often proposed as guiding values. I invite you not to take the mantra "sustainability" too seriously, even though it is widely accepted and also included in UN declarations. It has no clear meaning and is open to contradictory interpretations, which make that term convenient for demonstration consensus when none exist. Also, it suffers from too many ambiguities and carries "conserving" connotations which do not fit an epoch of radical transformations. What should be "sustained": present standards of living? Birth rates? Accelerating science and technology? Global stocks of coal underground? All living species? Or perhaps the very nature of humanity as being an ephemeral entity in accord with the usual processes of evolution?

7.9 Similarly, I recommend to be wary of "happiness" as a proposed value to be served by humanity-craft. Happiness is a slippery subjective feeling the nature of which largely depends on cultural assumptions. Thus, sacrificing one's life for a faith can make a true believer happy, when compared with having a lot of "good time" with sex, food, and company, which is the essence of "happiness" of many contemporary humans. And what about Soma in Aldous Huxley's *Brave New World?*

Or total immersion in virtual realities?

7.10 Therefore, "making people happy" is not proposed as part of the value compass of an HSG. As the term "human flourishing" by itself is not more useful, I suggest a revised version of the Greek idea of *Eudaimonia*, namely "self-realization," to be facilitated by HSGs, as discussed in Section 18. But this too is problematic and does not foreclose other meanings of "thriving" as preferred by different persons in diverse cultures—as long as these do not bring about catastrophes and definitely do not pose risks to the long-term existence of the human species.

7.11 In any case, what you as an HSG should strive to assure is the opportunity of future generations to exist and shape what they regard as a thriving life, while in turn providing future generations with similar opportunities.

7.12 Concerning the "hot" issue of human behavior toward animals, as noted the proposed basic norm leaves space for a human duty to minimize animal suffering and especially of intelligent ones, but does not dictate it. Instead, in cases of conflict, the proposed basic norm gives priority to the welfare of human persons and all the more so the future of the human species, even when this involves causing animal suffering. This poses hard issues of "proportionality." But in principle human duties toward animals (a better formulation from the perspective of the philosophy of law than "animal rights") are of lesser normative weight than the welfare and future of humanity. I know many will strongly disagree with this position, but I think that as an HSG you have to accept it.

7.13 The proposed basic norm leads to a mainly consequential ethics related to utilitarianism, in contrast to deontological ethics that judges the morality of an act in terms of adherence to moral values, independent from consequences. Consequentialism justified the use of morally doubtful and also immoral means when essential for achieving higher-value goals. But many questions remain open, such as on "just war"—which in any case is a largely outdated concept as it does not apply to escalating collisions with enemies of humanity who ignore all rules.

7.14 The basic norm serves as a meta-ethics on the basis of which more operational values and goals can, and need to be formulated, which in turn serve as a normative compass for composing and applying humanity-craft. A tentative hierarchy of such values and goals puts the basic norm at the top. Then come the reduction of catastrophes and lessening Hell on Earth, and so on.

7.15 Applying the basic norm and its derivatives in given contexts involves many tragic choices. Making them is one of the heaviest burdens and most serious responsibilities of you as an HSG. They require from you many moral virtues and full exertion of your moral reasoning and feelings. You can and should be assisted by spiritual advisors and take into account the opinions of compeers; and, with time, an emerging "humanity general will." But the final responsibility for the morality of your choices is yours and yours alone.

8. Humanity-Craft

8.1 Seriously composing humanity-craft requires as yet lacking knowledge and philosophic reflection. Also needed are full-scale global think-tanks devoted to developing humanity-craft, an expanded and diversified global epistemic community advancing relevant knowledge, novel humanity-craft professionals, and other relevant knowledge producing and policy designing institutions and persons. Above all, required are in your mind the qualities of a humanity-craft maestro. But all these are only tools for producing and implementing humanity-craft, which in turn is an instrument for realizing the basic norm and its secondary values and goals.

8.2 Please note my use of the term "composing" in respect to humanity-craft, instead of "making," "designing," "planning" etc. I do so because the meanings and associated feelings of the term "composing" are richer. They include not only pondering, but inspiration, creativity, artistic sense, intuition, "feel" and more. All these are required for arriving at optimal humanity-craft principles and constitute necessary processes in your mind as an HSG and in the minds of all humanity-crafting professionals.

8.3 The tentative humanity-craft principles which will be briefly presented include: (1) curbing ultra-dangerous capacities; (2) neutralizing enemies of humanity; (3) minimizing recklessness endangering humanity; (4) limiting human enhancement; (5) containing creeping dangers; (6) reducing Hell on Earth; (7) exploring the inconceivable; (8) bridging ruptures; (9) extending self-realization opportunities; (10) transvaluation; (11) laying foundations; and (12) global governance.

8.4 Please try and assimilate in your mind that the prime task of humanity-craft is to prevent catastrophes and especially threats to the existence of humanity. Most contemporary public and policy issues, such as conventional terror, inequality, and some impairment of human rights, are below the threshold of "endangering the long-term ex-

istence of the human species and extremely large-scale catastrophes."
Therefore, they belong to the missions of "ordinary" political leaders
including HSGs acting in such a capacity, but they are not a part of
your Promethean mission nor a subject for humanity-craft.

8.5 Focusing on fateful issues is essential for being an HSG, otherwise
the Promethean mission will be diluted and also displaced by important, but not fateful concerns. However, this raises serious difficulties.
There are many in-between issues. But the main problem is posed by
public demands which mainly concentrate on concrete current issues
rather than worries about the future of humanity.

8.6 As long as immature public opinions dominate the political arena,
HSGs often have no choice other than hiding their humanity-craft
endeavor behind a screen of doing what matters to the public. Enlightening them on what really makes a big difference is essential, but
difficult, takes much time, and may require the harsh teachings of catastrophes. Till then, trusting a "public sphere," or an internet "town
gathering", as proposed by some reality-ignoring political theorists,
regretfully cannot be recommended to you.

9. Deep Sources of Fatal Dangers

9.1 Let me illustrate the already presented thesis of humanity being
ensnared in an evolutionary trap in action, because it reveals the deep
sources of fatal dangers with which humanity-craft has to cope. An
article which I read in April 2017 provides an opportune entry into
the subject. It described the escalating arms competition between the
USA and Russia, with the United States considering novel kinetic

energy projectiles to counter possible nuclear warhead firing capacities of the novel Russian T-14 Armata tank. This looks and is crazy, but well illustrates some of the main drivers of human evolution becoming more and more of a possibly deadly trap, namely envy, seeking of power, competition, search for enemies, and warfare.

9.2 These motives accompany human evolution together with a lot of mutual learning and cooperation, but the many books which emphasize the latter as being more pronounced are biased. Both a lot of hostility and quite some collaboration were essential for humanity reaching its present cultural, socio-economic and scientific–technical relative high levels. But because of the increasingly destructive power of humanity, continuation of the same evolutionary dynamics increasingly causes catastrophes and may lead to self-elimination of humanity as a species.

9.3 Human progress had a high price. There exist no knowledge and tools which humanity has not used for conquest, enslaving, maiming, and killing. However most dangerous of all as potentially destroying humankind is the deep propensity imprinted on humanity to be willing and also eager to engage in self-righteous mass-killings.

9.4 Humans need a faith to provide them with self-understanding, give meaning to being and death, and guide their lives. But believing in one faith often stamps believers in other faiths as "evil" or at least "ignorant," it being often regarded as a moral duty to teach them better or kill them. Thus, the conscience of the leading Nazis was clean: they sincerely believed that killing all Jews is necessary for protecting the superior Aryan civilization and taking care of the future of "real humanity" against dangerous sub-humans.

9.5 Multiple forms of greed and related desires and emotions also fulfilled a major role in making much of human history into a tale of misery and continue to do so with vigor. But it is the self-righteous mass-killings which support Hegel's view of human history as a "slaughter-bench." Adam Smith hit a crucial truth when he wrote in his important but neglected book *The Theory of Moral Sentiment* (1759) "of all the corruptions of moral sentiments factions and fanaticism have always been by far the greatest." Sliding from faith to fundamentalism, from fundamentalism to fanaticism, and from fanaticism to self-righteous mass killings—come naturally to much of humanity, especially when under stress and given charismatic and toxic (in our view) leaders.

9.6 Greed can also lead to human-caused catastrophes, as can errors, accidents, lack of foresight, ressentiment, competition for essential resources, hatred, gross negligence, and "bad luck," But self-righteous fanatics pose the major danger. Paradoxically, self-righteous fanatics are also essential for advancing what most of humanity at a given time regards as "true values", putting the human species into a tragic "catch" which becomes increasingly dangerous with the availability of increasingly effective mass-killing instrument. Thus, fanatically believing in human rights was essential for eliminating slavery, but tragically-paradoxically this required a very bloody Civil War in the USA.

9.7 You as an HSG must fully understand the root problem of major dangers to the future of humanity: **Intrinsic to the very nature of values as accepted by humans is collision between value systems regarding as absolute evil what other value systems regard as highly moral —leading quite easily to a subjective highly moral sense of duty to kill others up to readiness to die in order to do so.**

9.8 Imagine a sect believing sincerely that it is its moral duty to speed up Apocalypse in order to bring about the Second Coming of the Savior. They intend to do so by trying to kill all humans, including themselves, with the help of a mutated virus which bioengineer members of the sect can synthesize. Given the history of humanity, the possibility of such fanatic sects emerging cannot be denied. Given advances in bioengineering the likelihood of being able to prepare such a virus in a kitchen laboratory is likely to increase.

9.9 To better imprint such possibilities on your mind, I will share with you a few additional examples of the human sources of fatal dangers. Let us assume that it becomes possible to produce a nano-robot type which easily enters human bodies. If equipped with a self-reproducing algorithm it can kill most of humanity, but under controlled conditions it immunizes humans against all forms of cancer. Possible scenarios of consequences include the following:

- A laboratory produces the nano-robot for medical use and equips some of them for economic reasons with a self-reproducing algorithm. All this is done under maximal security conditions. But a human error, or a surprising mechanical malfunction, releases faulty nano-robots which kill about 30% of humanity.

- A group of hyper-green activists are true believers in their moral duty to eliminate humanity so as to save Gaia from greedy destruction. It steals some nano-robots from medical facilities, equips them with self-reproducing algorithms together with mass-killing instructions and releases a few such nano-robots simultaneously at 10 main airports. As they expect, all the activists die, but so do 80% of humanity accompanied by breakdown of the global socio-economic scientific–technological civilization.

- An African state mired in poverty sets up a hidden nano-engineering facility which produces mass-killing self-reproducing nano-robots. Some of them are hidden by a number of highly committed government agents in five capital cities of main powers. The ruler of the state sends examples of the nano-robots to the United Nations and declares that the rich Western countries owe reparations to the poor African state for years of enslavement and plundering, at the rate of 10,000 trillion US Dollars at its present purchase power, to be paid over 10 years by the USA and Western European countries as they may decide. If they refuse this just demand, the mass-killing nano-robots will be released worldwide. The note ends with the statement "We prefer our death to continuing miserable existence caused by Western avarice and murderous imperialism." The note, with samples of "dead" nano-robots proving its availability, is sent next day to main global mass-media.

9.10 There is much more to say on the deep sources of dangers posed by humanity to humanity, but the discourse above should be adequate to clarify what you have to deal with. Never mind if you regard some of the examples farfetched. The main point is beyond dispute: **It is not science and technology that endanger humanity, but humans producing, marketing, using and misusing them as they are increasingly likely to do. Therefore the mantra "saving humanity from itself" sums up the core of your Promethean mission and the task of humanity-craft.**

9.11 A quote from psychohistorian Erik H. Erikson in his book *Life History and the Historical Moment* (1975) sums up what you as an HSG face:

"Man as a species cannot afford any more to cultivate illusions either about his own 'nature' or about that of other

species, or about those 'pseudo-species' he calls enemies—
not while inventing and manufacturing arsenals capable of
global destruction ...”

9.12 Erikson presented this opinion fifty years ago. It becomes increasingly pertinent with the accelerating development of increasingly
lethal knowledge and tools. An HSG cannot permit himself such de-
lusions as believing in a fundamentally "good" human nature, though
I do not urge you to move to the other extreme of believing in a fundamentally "evil" human nature. Rather I recommend as your working
assumption the assessment that humans can easily be "good" or "evil,"
depending on how we understand these concepts, circumstances, leadership, and historic as well as random factors.

9.13 Do not be fooled by widespread pop-psychology. It is not true
that frustration, ignorance, and destitution are main factors producing self-righteous mass-killers. This happens and intense efforts are
required to reduce such effects. But this is only a part of the story.
Members of the Nazi elite, of fanatic terror cells, of doomsday sects,
and similar dangerous "true believers" entities include highly educated
and affluent activists, who feel duty-bound to engage in mass-killings,
sometimes up to a mentality of "either we win or humanity has no
right to exist." Certainly, Hitler would have used a doomsday instrument rather than let a humanity not dominated by Nazis exist.

9.14 Given that the root cause of large-scale catastrophes, and perhaps
elimination of the human species, is humanity itself, the question is
what to do about it. Changing human nature is not a practical way to
reduce dangers to humanity, certainly not within the suggested time
horizon. "Education" and "enlightenment" hardly impact on basic human propensities. On the contrary, efforts to do so forcefully are often

counterproductive, as demonstrated by the history of revolutionary efforts, total education and "brainwashing. Some soulcraft may help, but this takes much time and cannot be relied upon. And efforts to engage in deep enhancement changing basic human values by gene-engineering, chemicals or other radical interventions may—if and when becoming feasible —easily cause grievous harm, such as repressing creativity. Therefore, at least within your time horizon, humanity-craft principles must focus on operational principles for reducing the dangers posed by humanity to itself. These are on a deeper level than "technical fixes" which are unlikely to work; but they are on a less deep level than the core nature of human beings, however understood or misunderstood.

10. Curbing Ultra-Dangerous Capacities

10.1 Given the difficulties of changing human propensities, the most basic humanity-craft principle is to prevent production and availability of ultra-dangerous capacities, including knowledge and tools which can cause catastrophes, meltdown of our civilization, and endanger the long-term existence of humanity.

10.2 This sounds obvious and promising, but is very difficult to accomplish and cannot fully succeed, for four main reasons:

(1) Unpredictability: what knowledge and tools are potentially ultra-dangerous. Thus, nanotechnology and quasi-intelligent robots may or may not have catastrophic, civilization meltdown, and even fatal consequences.

(2) Quite some knowledge and tools are, as mentioned, bi-

polar: they may be very beneficial and also potentially ultra-dangerous.

(3) Restriction of research and development may have overall bad consequences. It also seriously impairs human freedom and the market economy. Therefore, it is value-wise costly and will be strenuously opposed.

(4) To adequately enforce this humanity-craft principle strict prohibitions and restrictions have to be agreed upon by major powers, a global surveillance system has to be set up, an effective global intervention force will have to be established, and transgressors have to be hunted down and harshly punished (as enemies of humanity, discussed next).

But even if all these requirements are met, probably only after a major catastrophe, it still will be nearly impossible to eliminate islands of non-compliance.

10.3 Furthermore, stringent limitations on dangerous knowledge and tools not only foreclose many potential benefits, but they require radical changes in widely accepted values, and are themselves never fail-safe. Therefore, optimal limitations are much less than total prohibitions. Still, the evolutionary trap of humanity being capable of terminating its own existence, and probably tending to do so unless restrained, can in part be exited given optimal humanity-craft and much effort—including extensive regulation of production and diffusion of dangerous knowledge and tools. But, as already recognized, the evolutionary trap cannot be completely escaped. This conclusion is reinforced when all the other humanity-craft principles, as discussed in the following, are taken into account and integrated into a holistic view of their potentials and limitations.

10.4 Nature also poses partly unavoidable risks. Humanity-craft should include efforts to protect Earth from the impact of objects from space, such as asteroids, which can result in the extinction of humanity—on line with earlier extinctions of most of life on Earth. Early warning systems should be strengthened and more resources devoted to developing ways to change the trajectory of dangerous objects away from Earth. But this may be inadequate. Megathrust earthquakes (which involve deep layers of the surface of Earth) and supervolcano eruptions too can destroy humanity. Furthermore, some high-energy experiments may be worth doing despite a definite though probably minuscule risk of engulfing Earth and perhaps parts of the Cosmos.

10.5 Given the impossibility of completely preventing human-survival-endangering contingencies, or disproportional costs of doing so in terms of forgone benefits and impairment of values, last resort measures to save a sufficient number of humans to enable the species to recuperate and to safeguard for them advanced human knowledge are essential. These are best untaken by private foundations and individual philanthropists, as is the case to some extent, in addition to governments. A good example is the Norwegian Svalbard Global Seed Vault, but recent unexpected melting of permafrost and gushing of water into the tunnel leading to the vault illustrate the difficulties of doing so.

10.6 If advance warning is available, such as by tracking the trajectory of a large mass from space which cannot be diverted and that is likely to decimate most but not all of humanity, or slow expansion of areas hit by a killing virus which cannot be stopped, then urgent governmental and global emergency measures to assure species and civilization survival, even if most of humanity is killed, may become feasible, though probably secretly so. But as an HSG your best bet may often be encouragement of private initiatives, subject to oversight which forces them to take into account needs of the human species and not only their personal safety.

10.7 It may also become feasible to hedge against elimination of humanity on earth by seeding crucial masses of humans on moons and other planets of our solar system and perhaps, in the further off future, on exoplanets. Doing so also serves science and may provide materials or dumping places for human use. Beyond such utilitarian reasons, "up, up, and away" also satisfies human explorative and adventurous motives as well as curiosity as a main driver of human progress. Some might add a human mission to seed other planets with life, but I leave this for philosophers, theologians, and dreamy futurists to ponder.

10.8 Taking into account the recent view of Professor Stephen Hawking that the human species will have to populate a new planet within 100 years if it is to survive, as climate change, overdue asteroid strikes, epidemics and population growth make Earth increasingly precarious, and similar assessments by other distinguished scientists, devotion of large resources to space exploration and steps towards settling of humans beyond Earth are an important supplement of the presently discussed humanity-craft principle. Some parts of such endeavor can, as noted, be left to private initiatives. But the large scale of required efforts, which are unlikely to provide financial profits and carry considerable risks, make space exploration and perhaps settlement of humans beyond Earth necessarily into a governmental endeavor, preferably by a consortium of highly developed states and ultimately as a main project of global governance. As an HSG you should prepare the ground for such endeavors and strongly support them.

10.9 It is not clear if humanity can make itself into an exception from the ultimately ephemeral nature of all species, but this is a matter for the far off future. However in the short term too, the best human measures cannot fully guarantee survival of humanity, though they can significantly increase its likelihood. We will have to exist and evolve under the shadow of possible termination and quite some likelihood of catastrophes. This is not an insight to be advertised in mass-media nor to be discussed in schools. But you as an HSG should be aware of it, viewing all the more so humanity as existing on the edge of the unknowable, and doing your very best to reduce the likelihood of major catastrophes and especially the elimination of our species—unless deliberately chosen by humanity in order to let a higher species take over, already mentioned as a hypothetical far off possibility.

10.10 There remains the horrible question what to do if the elimination of humanity becomes inevitable, such as due to a large mass from outer space unavoidably colliding with Earth and sure to kill all of humanity. Should the public be informed of this coming disaster well in advance, or kept ignorant as long as possible? Should humans who want to kill themselves before disaster strikes be supplied with poison capsules? Should public order be maintained till the last moment and how can this be done? Should religious leaders be mobilized and provided with access to mass media to offer transcendental consolation?

10.11 As an HSG you should be aware of such questions. I would include them for consideration in a Seminary for HSGs. But they should not preoccupy you and surely you must not let them depress you.

11. Neutralizing Enemies of Humanity

11.1 Given the impossibility and also undesirability to clean Earth of ultra-dangerous knowledge and tools, many of which can also advance human thriving, the next crucial line of defending humanity is neutralizing "enemies of humanity." Reaching back to Roman law, which declared pirates to be *"hostis humani generis"* who should be apprehended and punished harshly wherever they are, this humanity-craft principle requires supplementation and enlargement of the category of "crimes against humanity" by adding the more extreme category of "enemies of humanity," to be hunted down, subjected to harsh interrogation, judged by special tribunals, and punished severely.

11.2 Despite the shock effects of "ordinary terrorism" and its disruptive and painful effects, it is a minor problem. The number of persons killed by car accidents is larger by orders of magnitude. Fear of terrorism impairs quality of life, but humanity got used to lethal epidemics and wars and continued to thrive. Up till recently terrorists and even fanatic states such as Nazi Germany could not endanger the future of humanity.

11.3 Is the situation changing and are enemies of humanity a catastrophic and also fatal threat, or is this a figment of wild imagination? The answer, regretfully, is that they are in the process of becoming a catastrophic and also fatal threat. Doomsday sects and fanatic regimes existed throughout history including recently. There is no doubt that Hitler would have used a doomsday weapon if he had one rather than let the enemies of Nazism triumph. The implications are ominous: **Enemies of humanity trying to kill many millions and perhaps seeking to terminate the existence of the human species, often regarding doing so as a moral duty, are a real danger and will increasingly be so for the foreseeable future. Therefore, their prevention and elimination is a top priority, however costly in terms of values and resources.**

11.4 Therefore the "ticking bomb" doctrine on extracting information needs expansion; preventive detention may sometimes be essential; "profiling" is likely to be unavoidable; uses of the Internet have to be monitored; and it may in some cases be less bad to convict some innocent persons on the basis of a preponderance of evidence, rather than let millions of humans and perhaps humanity as a whole be destroyed by clinging to the "beyond reasonable doubt" rule. Also, the death penalty may be justified against leading enemies of humanity, but I leave this to your judgment.

11.5 To be noted is the dramatic shift in the global geo-political situation resulting from the real possibility of minor states, and also small non-state actors, acquiring ultra-dangerous capacities and being willing to use them. The result is comparable kill-capacities by what were and still often are by all other criteria minor actors and superpowers. The concept "asymmetric warfare" becomes misleading. Peace-maintenance principles, such as "balance of power," "collective security," "mutual assured destruction," and so on have never been failsafe. But with fanatic minor actors capable of causing large-scale catastrophes and perhaps be willing to do so—widely accepted theories of international relations are undermined and become increasingly irrelevant and also misleading.

11.6 As ultra-dangerous knowledge and tools cannot be eliminated, inter alia because of the beneficial potentials of some of them, what remains is prevention and elimination of enemies of humanity who may be capable of acquiring ultra-dangerous capacities and willing to use them. This is impossible without a strict global security regime as part of a decisive global governance system, which is radically different from the United Nation as presently constituted and operating.

11.7 Whatever may be done, technologically-sophisticated fanatics feeling morally entitled and also obliged to engage in mass-killings and perhaps to eliminate humanity, will remain a real danger. Deterrence does not work against those who are willing to die for their beliefs, radical measures taken against them will be met by fanatic countermeasures, driving the total collision ("war" is an inappropriate term) to extremes in a competition which the fanatics may well win.

11.8 The fact is that no amount of global surveillance can catch all fanatic groups willing to hit humanity before they acquire mass-killing and perhaps doomsday tools. Therefore, some risks for humanity inevitably remain if and when catastrophic and doomsday tools are within the reach of fanatic states, small fanatic groups, and perhaps even lonely fanatic actors.

11.9 Even the best HSGs using the most advanced technologies are unlikely to prevent all fanatic catastrophic mass-killings. Such failures, though unavoidable, will discredit political leaders and result in somewhat crazy voting behavior bringing to the top incompetent political leaders, who will cause more damage—leading under some circumstances into a vicious spiral. Preparing for such a dynamics, counteracting it as far as possible, and using resulting disruptions as opportunities to execute radical humanity-craft measures which are not feasible under ordinary circumstance, are main tasks of HSGs which require anticipation and preparation.

11.10 A special and very difficult case is posed by rulers, states, groups and also loners who "perhaps" are in the process of becoming enemies of humanity, Hitler being a prime example. Had the French moved forcefully against Hitler when he remilitarised the Rhineland in 1936 they would have been branded as "warmongers." There would be no

Hitler causing the Second World War, but no-one would know what was prevented.

11.12 Keep such cases in mind when trying to judge history or learning from specific historic episodes (as distinct from deep historic processes). You can never know what would have happened if some important events had taken a different form, as they usually could because of the contingency of history. So-called "virtual history" is an interesting form of thought experiments, which enlarge vistas. but not more. Therefore, precaution requires stern action against potential fanatic actors before they acquire significant kill-capacities, but this easily becomes a justification for a lot of counter-productive aggression which is not really justified.

11.13 The case of nuclear weapons supposedly possessed by Saddam Hussein and the dismal results of the Western invasion of Iraq in 2003 are striking examples of the dilemmas of trying to deal with "perhaps crazy actors who perhaps acquire catastrophic weapons." But we can only speculate on what might perhaps have happened if the Western invasion had not happened. Because of such and other deep uncertainties coping with potential enemies of humanity poses great difficulties and forces you to do a lot of "fuzzy gambling" for high stakes, as discussed in section 27.

11.14 You can read and reread Clausewitz and San Tzu as much as you like, but with the exception of some insightful philosophic contemplation they are irrelevant for security issues faced in the Anthroporegenesis epoch. A new grand-strategic paradigm, however urgently needed, has not yet been developed. Therefore, you have to ponder and act without the help of intellectual banisters, while pushing development of new theories fitting radically novel situations—such as posed by fanatic enemies of humanity.

11.15 Different but related are the very troublesome cases of legitimate heads of governments who are not "enemies of humanity" in the full sense, but choose tribal policies clearly bad for humanity, even if in the short run perhaps convenient for their countries. Examples come easily to mind. Such rulers of important states can cause a lot of damage to humanity, for instance to climate policies. It is the duty of all HSGs to act against such political leaders, but how to do so depends on specific circumstances.

12. Minimizing Recklessness Endangering Humanity

12.1 A power station uses coal emitting a lot of CO_2 which causes dangerous climate changes; a commercial enterprise legally sells mass-killing weapons; and a bioengineer develops a technique enabling mutation of viruses in kitchen laboratories. Are they morally to blame? I do not think so. The job of a power station is to produce electricity as cheaply as possible; a commercial enterprise is committed to maximizing legal profits for its owners; and bioengineers do their professional job in developing virus mutating technologies, all the more so if their intention is to heal cancer. As long as they act within the law none of the actors presented above are guilty of dereliction of duty or immorality.

12.2 Ethical theory includes the concept of "supererogation," which refers to desirable actions "beyond the call of duty." Public opinion often admires morally good acts that are not strictly required. But no effective system of ethics can be based on them, neither can humanity-craft. Not acting according to supererogation is not illegal, nor immoral, and cannot count as recklessness, negligence, or an error. Preventing, or at least reducing, behavior that becomes super-dangerous requires a clearly defined, targeted and enforced humanity-craft principle translated into detailed operational norms, codes and laws.

12.3 Accordingly, preventing mass-killing viruses escaping from laboratories, publication on the Internet of instructions on building nuclear weapons, burning tropical rainforests and so on—cannot be prevented and justly punished unless they are implicitly, explicitly or "obviously" contradicting accepted norms or/and formally forbidden. Therefore, it is important to develop and diffuse a humanity-protecting moral sense together with setting down clear codes of behavior having legal or other formal standing, or at least included in more or less commonly understood formulations such as "behavior fitting an officer;" and, in the future if crystalized and enshrined, "behavior fitting a bioengineer;" and, most importantly, "behavior fitting a political leader."

12.4 Given explicit or "obvious" duties, their unintentional but preventable breach constitutes negligence. If the safety of humanity is endangered, such negligence does not make the guilty parties into enemies of humanity, but the severity of consequences turns their negligence into recklessness deserving severe punishment. But, minimizing humanity-endangering recklessness requires, in addition to the measures detailed above, also (1) clarification of the scope of duties; (2) constant training and supervision; (3) surveillance; and (4) painful sanctions.

12.5 This is a very important point. Relying on good will is fine, but not enough. Expecting special caution when dangerous knowledge or materials are handled is morally justified, but not adequate. Really to minimize recklessness in handling ultra-dangerous stuff requires reinforcing motivation and a lot of automatic safeguards. But clear codes of conduct strictly enforced are also essential.

12.6 As clearly demonstrated by plenty of cases, humans are prone to err. And no mechanism can be completely fail-safe. The statement, "to err is human" is true. This returns us to the humanity-craft principle that scarcity of ultra-dangerous knowledge and tools is the ultimate safeguard against humanity-caused self-destruction. The propensity humans have to commit errors adds to the necessity to strictly limit the production and availability of dangerous knowledge and tools. This is a most important basis for human species security.

13. Limiting Human Enhancement

13.1 However vague the borderline is, I suggest distinguishing between "mild" and "hard" enhancement. Mild enhancement includes marginal changes in human attributes, such as some lengthening of life expectancy, increased immunity against diseases, and regeneration of organs. Hard enhancement would include, for instance, major increases of cognitive abilities, mental interface at a distance with computers and the Internet, and implanting of knowledge chips.

13.2 Minor enhancements may cause problematic social ruptures. Thus, raising life expectancy to 120 good-quality years may impact on birth rates, break all pension arrangements, lead to violent generational conflict, require institutionalized "second career" opportunities, change leisure patterns, and more. But such problems are manageable. They are unlikely to cause catastrophes or meltdown civilization and are very unlikely to stimulate doomsday fanaticism endangering the survival of humankind.

13.3 Much tougher, as already mentioned, are the moral, social, and political problems posed by radical life expectancy prolonging treatment, say up to 200 years, if very expensive so that only the extremely rich can afford it. I tend to the view that either the treatment should be available to all; or at least to all within well-defined categories which most of the public will accept as fair, such as Noble Prize recipients. Allocating some of the treatments by lot may also increase a sense of fairness.

13.4 Alternatively, it may be advisable, until such life-prolonging technology become more affordable, to strictly prohibit them also for geniuses—with black marketers and illegal buyers being prosecuted globally. Otherwise, humans not only become divided into two biologically castes, but basic values of fairness, and equal core rights are negated, with revolutionary violence using mass-killing tools being one of the possible consequences.

13.5 The same reasoning applies, with adjustments, to other hard enhancements, such as significant upgrading of mental capacities, doubling of bodily abilities and so on. The powerful will make strenuous efforts to benefit from such enhancements. And some states my engage in hard enhancement, for instance to gain scientific and military advantages. Reliance on professionals to adopt and keep a code of ethics limiting hard enhancement is of little help, if at all. Therefore, it will be difficult to get global agreement on what to prohibit; and global enforcement of agreed limitations may require drastic measures. I doubt if HSGs can do much about this danger before catastrophes open the door to needed measures globally enforced effectively.

14. Containing Creeping Dangers

14.1 Coping with creeping dangers poses many problems. Climate change is such a danger, likely to result in Hell on Earth and perhaps catastrophes, probably even earlier than expected as indicated by disintegration of parts of the Antarctic glaciers, but not extinction of humanity. Rapid population growth may also be a creeping danger, as it depletes natural resources, including water and agricultural land. Extreme growing inequality is a third illustration of creeping dangers.

14.2 Increasingly visible harsh consequences of climate change may drive global politics to take effective containment steps, though too late for preventing momentum-driven further climate-caused calamities. Population growth may engender Malthusian "natural" counter-processes, such as hard to handle lethal epidemics in densely populated underdeveloped countries. But science and technology may increase the carrying capacity of Earth despite predictions to the contrary. Also, net reproduction rates can be influenced by national policies, as illustrated by China. Thus, creeping dangers are usually not catastrophic and even less so fatal, unless they implode.

14.3 Still, they should be contained, to reduce suffering and prevent dangerous escalation. Ways to do so depend on the specifics of different creeping dangers. Thus, many ways have been proposed to contain damaging climate changes, though all of them are expensive and require changes in life styles and are therefore strenuously opposed.

14.4 Reducing birthrates so as to prevent the predicted large growth in human population from about 7.5 billion in 2017 to about 11 billion in 2100, with most of the growth taking place in underdeveloped Africa, requires strenuous efforts starting with intense education of women and supply of birth control means, up to strict one child family enforcement as was the case in China. But the creeping nature of population growth combined with intense religious and other opposition to birth reducing measures make containment difficult—so that harsh consequences, comparable to those of uncontained climate change, are likely.

14.5 Wealth inequality has been on the rise since 2008, with the top percentile of wealth holders now owning about 50% of all household wealth. The sixty-two richest billionaires own as much wealth as the poorer half of the world's population. While the rapid development of China and some other Asian countries reduces global inequality, the income and quality of life differences between humans in, for instance, Bangladesh and many African countries and Western states remains vast.

14.6 However bad this inequality is in moral terms, it seems not to endanger humanity. But this is a delusion. With the dramatic inequality becoming obvious also to the poorest strata, thanks to easier access to mass media and the Internet, explosions are likely—all the more so as very poor countries too can acquire new mass-killing instruments. The lesson from history that reshuffling of wealth is impossible without large-scale violence adds to the danger of catastrophes.

14.7 Suggestions for reducing extreme inequality abound, such as changes in tax structures together with closing of all tax havens and strict enforcement of tax laws. But, as wealth provides not only economic but also political power, and as the very wealthy as a rule want to preserve what they have and also to get more, contemporary politics is not really able to take the drastic steps required for reducing extreme inequality. Therefore, this is a creeping danger hard to handle without socio-political explosions. Revolutionary regime changes are not enough, as illustrated for instance by Venezuela. Needed are superb politicians who will know to reduce inequality without meltdowns, together with fear of violence motivating the very rich to agree to some capital redistribution as dictated by self-interest.

14.8 The same is more or less true for other creeping dangers, the insidiousness of which make them hard to handle before they change from "creeping" to "galloping" at high costs. The classical Chinese strategic rule to win a war before it starts is hard to apply. All that I can suggest to HSGs is to be alert to creeping dangers and use crises for coping with them.

15. REDUCING HELL ON EARTH

15.1 Using a variation of an apt term of Dag Hammarskjöld (he spoke about "preventing Hell on Earth"), reducing Hell on Earth is a priority humanity-craft principle, though less so than preventing catastrophes. As there is a lot of Hell on Earth, and as human beings have a propensity to produce more of it, all that may be feasible in the foreseeable future are serious efforts to reduce them.

15.2 There is significant progress in this needed direction, partly as a result of beneficial science and technology and partly as a result of global efforts, such as set forth in the United Nations Millennium Development Goals and the Sustainable Development Goals. But much more is needed, including stopping warfare; eliminating mass-killings; taking care of refugees, while reducing their number; eradicating still existing slavery; and putting an end to abject poverty.

15.3 Syria provides a tragic case of failure to prevent a harsh instance of Hell on Earth, from which much can be learned. Starting in 2011, by 2016 the number of killed by the so-called "civilian war" was around 250,000, with 4–5 million refugees. Misery in most of Syria is extreme. "Side effects" included temporary expansion of the Islamic State and plenty of violence in Iraq. The flow of refugees into Europe causes an upsurge in tribalism, with political leaders being at a loss what to do. Big power involvement carries additional serious dangers. In short, Syria is a paradigmatic case of failure to "prevent and protect," despite declarations and resolutions at the UN which had no effect whatsoever.

15.4 I may be biased by living near some Hell on Earth, but I know what I am talking about. Realization of the humanity-craft principle to reduce Hell on Earth requires forceful action, but the "global order" is incapable of doing what is relatively easy compared with most humanity-craft requirements. This bodes ill for the future.

16. Exploring the Inconceivable

16.1 Keeping within the realm of what is considered by reputable scientists as perhaps feasible within the time horizon under consideration, the following possibilities illustrate what may have to be coped with:

- Creation of life in laboratories, such as single cells and small multi-cell creatures.

- Recreation of select extinct species, called "de-extinction," or "resurrection biology," or "species revivalism," probably by some kind of quasi-cloning.

- Human cloning.

- Robots equipped with general artificial intelligence, leading perhaps the way to "spiritual machines."

- Radical enhancement of humans, moving toward Homo superior and/or cyberborgs (short for "**cyb**ernetic **org**anism")—beings with both organic and bio-electronic–mechanic and perhaps nanomachine body parts.

- Transmutation of materials thanks to molecular engineering.

- A breakthrough in fusion technologies, providing humanity with unlimited, cheap and non-polluting energy—but probably together with total doomsday weapons.

- Reception of "signals" from outer space making it very likely that intelligent beings exist on exoplanets.

- Genetic engineering which increases radically the intelligence of Chimpanzees.

- Reliable ways to "suspend" humans and reawaken them in an undefined future.

- Virtual worlds easily accessible on the Internet, providing a complete sense of reality in which many humans want to spend most of their lives as avatars.

- Easily produced "logic bombs"—a kind of mega-cyber-attack which can completely paralyze or distort all algorithms built into computers, robots, and other artificial systems on which modern civilization depends. Small groups of gifted hackers may be able to produce and use logic bombs, providing them with more power than the standing armies of major states.

16.2 I leave aside even more radical hypothetical possibilities, such as uploading human minds on nanocomputers, or visitors from outer space. But each one of the "inconceivabilities" above is enough to make Alvin Toffler's "future shock" into a mild cold when compared with the collective mental and social "brain stoke" likely to follow realization of possibilities as mentioned above. And such realization is quite likely within the foreseeable future unless ongoing research and technology development is selectively put on hold.

16.3 Evolutionary theories regard such developments as an extreme case of much accelerated "punctuated equilibrium," fitting the ideas of Stephen Jay Gould. Some theologians can view them as human participation in God-ordained creation. Philosophers may think that they prove teleological views of evolution, and so on. But such high-blown contemplations make no difference to public reactions. Most of humanity is likely to be thrown out of balance and lose faith in traditional beliefs—or cling to them more fundamentally. Self-understandings, meta-ethics, trust in science and technology, holiness of human life—these are only some of the foundations of modern humanity likely to be undermined by such mental earthquakes.

16.4 An optimistic outlook may foresee a new and higher level of human self-understanding and morality, following a relatively short crisis. But pessimistic outlooks may be more valid. Science and technology as a whole may be frozen. Disoriented fanatics may try to eliminate "sinfully hubris" humanity. And, at the very least, world-wide global turmoil is sure to cause extreme suffering.

16.5 Suspending research and technology development on most of the contingencies discussed above, till humanity is riper for them, may be a good idea. But I am aware that without some "enlightening" catastrophes such proposals will not get traction. Therefore, my short-term recommendation to HSGs is to closely monitor science and technology advancing in such directions and be ready to freeze them if this seems advisable and becomes feasible, probably following dramatic incidents. At the same time pondering on what to do about such possibilities and preparing ideas for trauma-containing soulcraft are tasks for closed enclaves of spiritual–cultural leaders, carefully selected humanistic thinkers, and prime HSGs—who, inconspicuously, may have to initiate such enclaves.

17. Bridging Ruptures

17.1 The concept "rupture" refers to significant crises sure to accompany the shift of humanity into the Anthroporegenesis epoch. In addition to radical social crises, on a deeper level primal anxieties going back to infancy are likely to be reactivated by shocks, such as the middle classes losing employment and joining the destitute when artificial intelligent robots take over many white collar jobs; or knowing that the very rich can buy many more years of life, while "normal" humans will die at a younger age. Therefore, I prefer the stronger term "rupture" instead of "crises" to refer to expectable breaks in the continuity of deep historic processes and widely held social norms and expectations.

17.2 Emergency treatment is needed and in part possible if prepared in advance. Essential are material help meeting basic needs; solidarity and fair sharing of sweat and blood; soulcraft elucidating ruptures as part of historic transformation for the better, instead of blaming "enemies;" concrete plans leading visibly to a better future; toughness to maintain law and order; and political and spiritual leadership providing guidance while sharing hardship as an obvious duty willingly fulfilled, not for shows on television.

17.3 In the longer run more important is rupture utilization for realizing more of humanity-craft. If well handled, ruptures can serve as creative destruction enabling to do what should have been done earlier but was undoable before because of the tyranny of the status quo. This is likely to be crucial for actualization of many of the humanity-craft principles, deserving therefore emphasis: **Important humanity-craft principles are likely to be unrealizable without the loosening of the bounds of reality by ruptures (and, much more costly, catastrophes). Preparing to utilize them as opportunities for necessary humanity-craft implementation is, therefore, an important task of HSGs.**

17.4 To prepare for what are largely unforeseeable contingencies and utilize them for the better, an HSG must be imaginative, willing to engage in hypothetical speculations and counter-factual thought experiments, and excel as an improviser. Also needed is readying of multiuse human and material resources, and keeping a relatively large staff of highly qualified crisis coping professionals. All this will be regarded as very wasteful, until and unless painful ruptures come and justify visibly the preparation. But such "reality stress tests" may or may not come, or may be beyond what was prepared for. This is a risk you must take, closely related to your choices being fuzzy gambles.

18. EXTENDING SELF-REALIZATION OPPORTUNITIES

18.1 As detailed in the next section, saving humanity from itself requires limitation of individual and research freedom, intrusive global surveillance, weakening of state sovereignty and other painful transvaluation. To offset them and enlarge individual, group, and societal liberties, as a "good" in itself, I suggest the humanity-craft principle of extending individual and group self-realization opportunities.

18.2 As indicated in Sections 7.9–7.10, it is not by oversight that I do not include "maximization of happiness" or of "pleasure" among the goals of humanity-craft. I have three reasons for doing so in addition to already mentioned ones: (1) no objective "idea" or "essence" of "happiness," "pleasure," and so on exists (signs on brain scans in pleasure centers are symptoms, not content); (2) making "happiness" and "pleasure" into the basis of values reduces humans to rather simple animals lacking higher meanings of life; (3) the optimal way to make more people happy is to diffuse in the atmosphere a chemical stimulating the pleasure centers in human brains so that they feel all the time very "happy," till all of humanity dies "happily." This surely is not what humanity-craft should serve.

18.3 Different and more important from the species perspective is the overly individualistic nature of focusing on subjective feelings as such. A counter-value, which in terms of the long-term thriving of humankind is more important, is "maximizing species utility" of individual behavior. But this by itself is too "collectivist." Needed is a humanity-craft principle which covers both individualistic and collective perspectives complementarily. This requirement is satisfied by the proposed principle of "extending self-realization opportunities."

18.4 Self-realization can be tied to materialistic and hedonistic individual desires, such as by living in polygamy, polyandry, and group families and establishing various forms of "strange" communities. As long as consenting adults are involved and no harm is caused to others, this enables participants to realize themselves in pleasure and company. But self-realization can also be achieved by artistic and scientific creativity, taking care of the sick, and exploring space. Such forms of self-realizing can have very high species utility.

18.5 The humanity-craft principle of extending self-realization opportunities opens the way to a variety of mixes providing more individual "satisfactions" as well as more "species utility." When necessary, providing more or less opportunities of different types can influence the composition of the mixes without impairing individual freedom more than necessary for the thriving of humanity.

18.6 But too rosy an image of complete harmony between "freedom of individual choice" and "taking care of the future of the human species" is misleading. Individuals cannot be permitted to choose becoming enemies of humanity, engage in prohibited research, resist some intrusive surveillance, and so on. All the more so, as mentioned, enlarging the scope of non-dangerous individual freedom is essential as a kind of "compensation" for necessary restraints. Thus, I tend to the view that humans should be entitled to decide when to die, with options for ways to terminate one's life to be provided to all "choice-able" adults after an obligatory "reconsideration" period. You may agree or disagree with this particular view, but the principle to extend self-realization opportunities which do not endanger others is, I think, compelling— otherwise necessary restraints will be intolerable.

18.7 Enlargement of self-realization requires providing many options to all, such as schooling, reasonable travel, advanced studies, some forms of soft enhancement etc. Obviously, adequate satisfaction of material needs comes first. This leads to a revised version of "human rights" as including an assured minimum income subject to fulfillment of basic civic duties, such as perhaps devoting a number of years to obligatory "humanity-service."

18.8 It is likely that detachment from traditions and much more freedom to choose how to live may overtax the emotional capacities of many humans, increase existential anxiety, lead to nihilism, and cause mental breakdown. Therefore, self-realization opportunities should be expanded slowly, with more of them being offered to those who seek them; but not to be "thrown" on those not eager for them.

18.9 Extending self-realization opportunities raises even more difficult issues, such as free choice of religions, atheism or agnosticism. For a person to really have free choice by what faith to life, as long as it is not aggressive toward others, the right of parents to "educate" their children and social pressures must be reduced. Opportunities to explore different belief systems, and the right to live in communities supporting a chosen faith, have to be provided.

18.10 Handling such issues is value-wise problematic and politically nearly impossible. I think they should in the foreseeable future be left to states, regional civilizations, religions etc. Still, even so, they add up to a socio-cultural transformation. Taking into account the scientific–technological and economic transformation wrought by the Anthroporegenesis epoch, a correlated socio-cultural transformation is unavoidable. But the time scales are different: the scientific–technological and economic transformation is much faster. And trying to accelerate the socio-cultural transformation involves dangerous revolutionary processes which can easily be counterproductive, as shown throughout history.

18.11 Pinning one's hope on a rapidly emerging age of real enlightenment and maturation of humanity is a chimera, at least within the time horizons of the Memo. Therefore, the net result of the proposed humanity-craft principle is likely to be a mixed blessing: a growing gap between thinking, creative, high-culture, and science-and-technology sophisticated elites on one side; and, on the other side, a majority seeking the ordinary pleasures of life with some extensions.

18.12 This does not imply emergence of a new "underclass." If well managed then the Anthroporegenesis can with time supply a high standard of living for all in terms of good housing and food, a range of family life formats, company, sex, amusement, excitement, celebrities to admire and imitate, some sense of prevailing fairness, soft enhancement etc. It is your job as an HSG to provide more of these goodies to choose from by increasing parts of humanity, while extending "higher" self-realizing opportunities, largely supplied by free markets, academia, creators, spiritual leaders and private initiatives, to all able and willing to use them.

18.13 This is the proposed meaning of "fairness" recommended to you, together with the restraint of extreme wealth inequality as discussed. As an HSG you should do your best to realize such "fairness" in providing extended self-realization opportunities, knowing that this is a long and difficult process that can unfold only in phases, with ups and downs and, regretfully, accompanied by a lot of hopefully not very bloody social conflict.

19. TRANSVALUATION

19.1 Required changes in values, as indicated throughout the Memo, add up to extensive transvaluation which often rejects what is presently regarded as nearly sacrosanct. In this respect Friedrich Nietzsche was prescient when writing his book *Beyond Good and Evil: Prelude to a Philosophy of the Future* (1886). Not only public opinion but also much of political and moral philosophy needs revision to fit the requirements of global surveillance, limitations on research and technology, censorship of the Internet and public speech, severe treatment of enemies of humanity, limitation of state sovereignty in favor of decisive global governance and much more, including advancing the nature of the human species as a moral-deliberative agency and moving toward quality politics, as discussed in the two following sections. You as an HSG should call for such rethinking, lay on the table what is essential for saving humanity from itself, and follow closely salient deliberations.

19.2 To put needed transvaluation into perspective, consider the ongoing dramatic changes in sexual norms, largely produced by social processes without benefit of "command authority." Though often opposed, they changed the hegemonic global culture. The transvaluations required for saving humanity from itself are not much more radical and far from being "impossible." But they conflict with strong traditions and transgress widely accepted norms. Therefore, similar to other humanity-craft principles, it may take the shock of catastrophes to make them feasible. This is very probably the case, for instance, with establishment of urgently needed decisive global governance overriding on some issues state sovereignty.

19.3 From you as an HSG the needed transvaluation requires adjusting you own values and engaging a lot in "soulcraft," in the sense of convincing main social actors and large populations on the necessity to abandon some deeply held values and accept others instead. To succeed you need a lot of support, especially by a presently lacking globally respected spiritual leadership understanding what is at stake. Facilitating emergence of such leaders and cooperating with them while also learning from them, without intervening with their moral rethinking, is one of your tasks.

19.4 The few comments above, together with salient observations throughout this work, are far from doing justice to the scope and depth of the transvaluation essential for the continued survival of the human species and its thriving. What is really needed is a kind of "Second Axial Age," similar to but much faster than the Axial Age between 800 to 200 B.C.E., when Confucius, Buddha, Lao Tzu, and Zarathustra laid the foundations of a new civilization which continues to shape humanity. You, as an HSG, must recognize this need for a Second Axial Age, though its content is inconceivable. All you can try to do is clear parts of the way for humanity to make such a transformation, which will probably surpass by far the transition into the Anthropogenesis epoch however reality-shaking radical it is.

20. Laying Foundations

20.1 Humanity-craft composition and realization depend on the availability of actors and institutions able and willing to do so. Mobilizing, building, and activating them is a long-term process involving many agencies. But you should fulfill a key role in laying the necessary foundations. Doing so involves: (1) strengthening the nature of humanity as a moral-deliberative agency; (2) humanity-craft directed research, teaching, contemplation, and policy composing; (3) crystalizing a *Homo sapiens* guidance cluster; (4) moving toward quality politics; and (5) advancing toward effective global governance. One to four will be discussed in this section, but global governance requires a section of its own.

20.2 Modern philosophy and social sciences deal a lot with "agency" in the sense of conscious deliberating and planning entities. When an agency thinks in terms of "ought" it is called a "moral agency." Literature increasingly recognizes cooperative and collective agencies, such as corporations and states. But as yet the human species is not considered as a composite-collective moral-deliberative agency with intentionality, though thanks to globalization and emergence of rudimentary global governance there is some movement of reality in this direction.

20.3 Making the human species into more of a composite-collective moral-deliberative agency is essential for fully legitimized critical humanity-craft choices. At present, such choices are made by agents who somehow feel entitled, and in a few cases are partly authorized, to make decisions for and on behalf of the human species, though without future humanity having a voice. But, with the exceptions of leaders of global governance bodies, no one is formally charged with acting on behalf of (contemporary) humanity. This poses problems also for you as an HSG, to which I will return.

20.4 If we want critical choices shaping the future of the human species to express the preferences of the adult humans living at any given time (which is a big "if"), a number of possibilities are hypothetically open: direct decisions by humanity, such as by global referenda; selection, such as by global elections, of political humanity leaders who will make the choices; crystallization of a "general humanity will" on which choices can be based; and reliance on political leaders of states to act for humanity as a whole, such as at the United Nations. But none of these options can work given the present state of political leaders, humanity and the global order. Therefore, taking care of the future of humanity is largely neglected, with some important but narrow exceptions.

20.5 Till the global order is transformed, the future of humanity, as far as depending on humans at it increasingly does, is shaped by a mix between a variety of self-regulating socio-economic and scientific–technological processes, self-appointed care-takers of humanity, a variety of socio-economic power holders, and political leaders of states. However, none of them can be relied upon to save humanity from itself. In fact, they are certainly unable, and in part unwilling to do so. Thus, most political leaders of the prevailing types are in the main tribal and therefore constitute more of a grave problem as far as the future of humanity is concerned than a solution. And self-regulating processes, such as free markets and science and technology, impact mainly unintentionally and in part increasingly dangerously on the future of humanity.

20.6 As probably is clear to you, a minuscule part of humanity exercises dominant influence on choices impacting on the future of humanity as a whole. Such future-impactors somewhat depend on support by voters and other selectors, are confined by a variety of constraints, and subjected to many pressures. But still:

Though often denied, largely hidden, a "taboo" truth, but also obvious, a very minute part of humanity exerts most of the influence on the future of generations to come as far as it depends on humans, as it increasingly does.

20.7 This will not change in the foreseeable future, despite facades presenting a different picture and occasional breakthroughs of "public opinion," not necessarily for the better. But what can and must change are (1) inadequate commitment by many future-impactors to the long-term future of humanity, being instead preoccupied by tribalism, profits, curiosity etc.; (2) gross under-qualification of political leaders for taking care of the future of humanity; (3) lack of large publics enlightened on the critical issues of humanity and exerting collectively desirable influence on the minute part of humanity largely shaping critical choices.

20.8 The proposed genre of HSGs is designed to partly overcome weaknesses one and two. But overcoming the third very serious weakness requires much effort by HSGs, together with other enlightening future-impactors, to advance the nature of humanity as a composite-collective moral-deliberative agency—with increasing parts of humanity thinking in terms of "we, human being, with me being a part of the chain of generations," rather than "I," "citizen of country X, believing in religion Y," and all too often "we" as self-glorifying referring to a hypertrophied "I."

20.9 Doing what you can to enlighten humanity on its predicaments and engaging in soulcraft to upgrade shared deliberation on human issues are essential. Taking an active soul-crafting part in Internet discourse can be one of the steps in the needed direction. But all these are, as Mao Zedong put it, "only the first step in a long march"—and not necessarily in the right direction.

20.10 While the vast majority of humanity, including most of its leaders, continues to be ignorant about the critical challenges facing humanity and also largely captives of tribalism, you have to ignore public opinions and do, after consulting with some of the few who under-stand the challenges, what you think is best. This necessitates some core qualities of your mind, including a well-equipped "inner citadel" and a lot of *Sapere Aude*, as taken up in Sections 22 and 23. Also essen-tial is, as already mentioned, some camouflaging of what you really do, which, however undesirable, is fully justified by consequentialist eth-ics—as you must not let widespread tribalism and ignorance endanger your Promethean mission as an HSG.

20.11 Urgently needed as well are humanity-craft directed research, teaching, contemplation, and policy composing. Their scarcity is cry-ing to heaven. There exists a humanity-craft epistemic community in the making. But interests are unevenly divided between main issues. They tend to focus on climate change and on "terror" threats, but ne-glect the broad spectrum of challenges facing *Homo sapiens*. Therefore, strenuous efforts are needed to diversify, increase and also integrate the humanity-craft epistemic community in-the-making.

20.12 There are objective difficulties hindering doing so. Real inter-disciplinary study and teaching is inherently hard to achieve; training of humanity-craft professionals requires a demanding combination between theoretic knowledge, empiric research, and supervised prac-tical experience. Humanity-craft as a whole is far from being recog-nized as a legitimate scholarly and professional domain. And relevant texts and case studies are very scarce. Furthermore, the demand for humanity-craft professionals is as yet small. Nevertheless, attracting top quality students to such a challenging profession should not be very difficult.

20.13 Mostly in need of highly qualified humanity-craft professionals are HSGs. Without having such advisors even a best-intended and fully qualified HSG cannot accomplish much. Therefore, you should strongly support preparation of humanity-craft professionals, help to set up fitting university programs, mobilize money for research, provide internship opportunities, and offer attractive advisory positions near you.

20.14 What you need most are good humanity-craft ideas. These are best provided by a full-scale think tank of the RAND Corporation type fully devoted to humanity-craft composing. There are a number of university centers, research institutes, brains trusts and foundations doing useful work on parts of humanity-craft. But none, as far as I could find out, has the required critical mass of highly qualified, full time, interdisciplinary, and multi-experience staff who should characterize the recommended think tank, to be established by you and your compeers.

20.15 Moving on to the global guidance cluster, needed at its core is an HSG's network for shared thinking and mutual support. It should also include carefully selected scientists and technology developers, spiritual and social leaders, entrepreneurs, artists and authors, mass media pundits, and free-floating intellectuals. I am thinking on an order of magnitude of a few hundreds, from all civilizations, many under the age of 45, and about half being women.

20.16 This needs delicate handling, so as to avoid the image of a clique out to rule the world. Organized as a "Global Humanity-Craft Academy," formal and informal meetings, intense personal contacts, shared workshops and retreats, intranet, and similar interaction opportunities can serve to build up the cluster in bits and pieces.

20.17 It may well be advantageous to have an independent sponsor, such as a global public interest foundation or a university graduate humanity-craft school. But these are details to be fitted to opportunities.

20.18 Even the best of HSGs cannot escape from politics. A sage or saint may stand apart, but not an HSG. Furthermore, politics as a whole unavoidably plays a major and often critical role in advancing or retarding the composing and applying of humanity-craft. Therefore, your Promethean mission depends on the quality of politics worldwide, and especially in the major powers. Working hard to upgrade the quality of politics wherever you can is, accordingly, a main foundation-laying task of yours. What to do depends on situations and regimes. For democracies the following suggestions illustrate ways to upgrade politics, with other measures fitting different regimes, which may be preferable in different civilizations and situations:

- Full disclosure by leading election candidates of education, public service record, other work experiences, family finances, health, and more.

- Three real-time television-broadcasted rigorous examinations of leading political candidates by independent panels of academics and experts as well as some randomly selected citizen, including young ones, on main public issues, local, and global.

- National and international workshops and seminars for political leaders on main humanity issues. These should be strictly off the record, so as to encourage frank discourse. But publishing lists of participants may encourage participation.

- Every 5 years of serving as a member of a government or parliament, a 1 year sabbatical devoted to study and gaining experience in other countries or global governance, with all expenses, including family, fully covered. Return to the former position is to be guaranteed.

- Submission of an annual report of activities by members of parliaments and governments to the public should be obligatory, to be fact-checked by an independent audit office.

- Strict enforcement of a serious code of ethics.

- Extensive research and professional advisory services supplied to members of parliaments and similar bodies.

- Published registration of lobbyists with full information on whom they represent, personal background, and payment.

- Limitation of election costs and of direct or indirect contributions to candidates and parties, with certified accounts to be published, in order to contain and with time reduce the political power of wealth.

- Perhaps most important of all, establishment in all major countries of merit-based Senates, composed of scientists and scholars, to be selected by a mixed committee of former heads of governments and outstanding scientists and thinkers appointed by the head of the supreme court of a given jurisdiction. This Senate should primarily serve as an advisory body with most of its suggestions to be widely publicized. But it should have the authority to delay legislation and parliamentary decisions; and, with a special majority, to call, after a fixed minimum interval, special referenda. Self-dispersal of the Senate by a two-thirds majority of members should automatically result in new general election of the legislative representative bodies.

- To get even more adventurous, it might be good to experiment with selection of a small percentage of the members of a parliament by lot from among all adult citizens. And to enforce a quota of members below the age of 40.

20.19 I have in my head even more radical ideas, based in part on integrating neo-Confucian thinking on merit-based politics with Western representation theories, as discussed in a growing body of literature. A minimum, relatively easy to implement, and at least somewhat useful move in the needed direction is the establishment of a Global Leadership Seminary which political leaders are obliged to attend for a couple of months before taking office; and in elections to parliaments and similar bodies, a double vote by citizen below the age of 40 or having graduate university education. But I cannot in good conscience recommend to you to publicly support such "wild" ideas before the time is ripe.

20.20 Hopefully, the proposals make at least one point: the quality of politics can be improved without endangering democracy or other preferred political regimes, with the exception of evil ones which should be deconstructed. However, do not fool yourself. Most political leaders of the prevailing type will resist such reforms which are likely to deprive them of their positions, doing all they can to obstruct your efforts and, if they can, get rid of you. Take care!

21. GLOBAL GOVERNANCE

21.1 Laying foundations for limiting state sovereignty and empowering a decisive global governance system are supreme challenges facing HSGs. Substantive progress depends on catastrophes demonstrating glaringly the obsolescence of the present global order. Post-catastrophe realities will determine what kind of global regime will emerge, ranging from an oligopoly of major powers to a kind of curbed, hopefully benevolent, but at least partly authoritative Global Leviathan.

21.2 In the meantime, you should do your best to strengthen existing global governance structures, especially the United Nations and its agencies. If you have standing in Europe, buttressing a reformed European Union is a step in the right direction. And do facilitate thinking on alternative forms of global governance able to save humanity from itself, so that ripe ideas will be available when the clock of dire need, which is also the time of opportunity, strikes.

21.3 Some comments may help you do so. The catch phrase "think globally, act locally" is largely misleading. The human species is dispersed all over the world. Therefore "think globally and act globally" comes first when the future of humanity is at stake. Thus, limiting development and uses of dangerous technologies and neutralizing doomsday fanatics are only effective if enforced globally.

21.4 An expanded subsidiarity principle is appropriate. Issues should be handled at the lowest level of social institutions that is capable of doing so, including local governments and cities, bottom-up initiatives, social initiatives and private enterprises. States will continue to fulfill crucial functions. It is neither feasible nor necessary or desirable to move towards cosmopolitanism in its full sense of all of humanity becoming one global state. But providing directives, setting of criteria, oversight, and override authority have to be reserved for global governance and, when necessary, imposed by it.

21.5 When dangers to humankind stem from local situations, local countermeasures may be adequate. Thus, as nearly all rainforests are located in the Amazon River basin of South America, Indonesia, and the Congo Basin, action by four to five states and agencies might be enough for preserving them as an important resource of humanity. But relevant countries are unlikely and in part unable to do so without being motivated, pushed, helped, monitored, and compensated by global and other actors.

21.6 It may be enlightening to conclude this section with some words on greenhouse gas emission, though you may know it all. The United States and China together emit about 45% of the global total. Therefore, it is technically reasonable to focus efforts on reducing first of all emission by these two countries. But there is a big catch: in 2016 The United States emitted about 17 metric tons of CO_2 per capita annually and China about 7. Therefore, in negotiations on global climate change agreements, China and other countries with low per capita emission claim that equity requires to let them develop and emit more greenhouse gases while the United States and other highly developed countries with large per capita greenhouse gas emissions should significantly reduce them.

21.7 This means, given present technologies, that life styles in many highly developed and also powerful countries would have to be changed significantly, which will be resisted strenuously by most of their populations. Various devices for moving ahead in reducing greenhouse gas emission despite such fundamental disagreements, such as trade in emission permits, may help a little but are far from adequate. No wonder that the global politics of reducing greenhouse gases emission is overall a failure.

21.8 I mention this relatively straightforward and well-studied case to demonstrate that the present world order cannot deal adequately with global issues. What if containing population growth is necessary? How to cope with small countries developing biological weapons endangering large parts of humanity? Why are tax havens not closed down, as a minimal step to lessening inequality? What about reducing hell in Syria and taking care of its refugees?

21.9 It is crystal clear that emerging fateful issues facing humanity as a species require global measures which conflict frontally with prevailing tribalism, "national interests," state sovereignty, the fiction of state equality, and also capital-based power—not to speak about various nationalistic, "limited government," "anti-global governance" and similar obsolete and in part also reactionary ideologies.

21.10 Willing cooperation and distributed responsibility are desirable and important, but cannot be relied upon when the future of humanity is at stake. Scientists may agree to follow an impressive code of professional ethics, but a few are sure to break it. Countries may sign a global covenant on stopping development of killer robots, but some of them are likely to secretly seek an advantage. Global companies may promise not to market risky knowledge and tools, but some are sure to seek an extra profit by doing so. Therefore, a radical transformation of the "world order" is increasingly needed.

21.11 Within the time horizons of this Memo, cooperation of the willing, in line with the ideas of Immanuel Kant, may help but will prove inadequate. **Without a radical transformation of the global order, including limitation of state sovereignty and establishment of a decisive global governance system qualified to make optimal humanity-craft decisions and equipped with the will and instruments to en-**

force them globally, humanity cannot be saved from itself. But it is very unlikely that the essential radical changes in global order can be achieved before massive catastrophes give a painful lesson to humanity and its leaders. Regretfully is seems that humanity needs the whip before acting to safe itself from itself.

21.12 Working out tentative plans for setting up an adequate global regime when sure-to-come catastrophes provide opportunities to do what should have been done before, may well be the best you can do, in addition to upgrading the United Nations as far as possible, which will maximally be much less than a minimum of what is essential.

22. Required Core Qualities of Your Mind

22.1 The best place to start is Max Weber's 1919 lecture on *Politics as a* Vocation, which you must read and reread. The post-war context was one of transformation, making some of his comments all the more pertinent. In particular, relevant for you as an HSG are, inter alia, the following qualities which Weber demands from those wishing to be political leaders: living for politics and not from it; being fully committed to politics as a "vocation," including in the sense of a "calling;" acting according to an ethics of responsibility for consequences, in some relation with an "ethics of commitment," making all of political leadership into an ethical endeavor; being fully mature, in the sense of ability "to scrutinize the realities of life ruthlessly, to withstand them, and to measure up to them inwardly;" understanding the crucial importance of power and force; taking "distance" from issues and oneself; and, on important issues, "reaching the point where he says, 'Here I stand, I can do no other'" (a famous quote from Martin Luther when starting the Protestant Reformation).

22.2 You need to develop the specific core qualities of mind essential for an HSG, in addition to those demanded by Max Weber and others that you should share with all serious political leaders (which I will not discuss in this Memo). Some of the special core qualities required for being an HSG have been mentioned or are obvious, such as appropriate time horizons, this-worldly frame, the will and ability to compose humanity-craft and build its foundations; and, above all, becoming a humanity-craft maestro. But five additional critical core qualities required by your mind in order to be an HSG have to be added: (1) *Sapere Aude*; (2) pondering in terms of human species evolution; (3) radicalism; (4) clinical pain-feeling concern; and (5) fuzzy gambling sophistication.

22.3 You may feel overwhelmed by all the required qualities. Indeed, as already emphasized, only a minute part of humanity has the potential to become an HSG, though it is impossible to know in advance who may be made of suitable material for becoming one of the few. But take into account that you do not have to be "perfect" in all of the required qualities, which is humanly impossible. Being "good" in most and very good in a few can compensate for being weak in others, if you are aware of what you lack and make up for it by leaning on carefully selected colleagues and advisors.

23. *Sapere Aude*

23.1 I borrow the term "Sapere Aude," which in Latin means more or less "dare to rely on your own pondering abilities," from Emanuel

Kant's 1784 prize essay on the meaning of "enlightenment." The opening paragraph of that essay is of profound importance for an HSG:

> "Enlightenment is man's emergence from his self-incurred immaturity. Immaturity is the inability to use one's own pondering ability, without the direction of another. This immaturity is self-incurred if its cause is not lack of understanding, but lack of resolution and courage to use it without the direction of another. The motto of enlightenment is therefore: *Sapere aude!* Have courage to use your own understanding!"

23.2 As an HSG you must think differently from "ordinary" political leaders, from what is written in most books and taught at most university courses, and from the vast majority of humans. Therefore, you need a lot of internal autonomy, which constitutes a kind of "inner citadel."

23.3 Let me at this opportunity warn you that being different can easily evoke a lot of hostility and prevent you from occupying positions enabling you to act as an HSG. Two contradictory strategies can help you cope with this danger: hiding the differences or emphasizing them as making you worthy of support. I like the second more, because it is truthful. But sometimes you may be forced to conceal what you really are. This leads to another essential quality in your mind, namely what the Greek called "metis," in a sense combining wisdom and cunning, as demonstrated by Odysseus—which is of much higher quality than the somewhat crude recommendations of Machiavelli in *The Prince*. But as all successful political leaders need it I do not discuss *metis* as one of the special qualities of an HSG.

23.4 Your internal autonomy needs constant expansion. Without it "freedom of will" means very little. Your mind should encompass increasing knowledge and understanding and be creative in developing novel ideas and new options. Daring to rely on your own pondering also requires a lot of reflection and contemplation. You need the ability to disconnect from pressing issues and let your mind play around with ideas, consciously and subconsciously. Being very curious is another essential building block.

23.5 Needless to say, but still worth saying, autonomous pondering without much knowledge is like pushing the gas pedal of a car without a gear. In contrast to most political leaders, you have to be conversant with the principles of science and technology; you should understand main human civilizations; you have to comprehend the processes of evolution as far as known; and much more.

23.6 Therefore, daring to rely on your own pondering does not mean being imperious to inputs. On the contrary, an HSG must constantly seek them. But as political leaders are overloaded with advice, requests, reports, meetings, rituals, and so on, your inner citadel needs discriminating door keepers who let in what is interesting and salient and refuse entry to all else.

24. Pondering in Terms of *Homo Sapiens* Evolution

24.1 Contemporary global civilization focuses on persons mainly as individuals, not as parts of collectives. And the human species as such is hardly a subject of discourse outside small though growing professional and some public groups. UN debates and declarations focus on individuals rights, not humankind. Therefore, pondering in terms of human species evolution may look strange and even dangerous to many. But you cannot look after the future of humanity without focusing on the evolutionary processes of the species.

24.2 The already mentioned concept of "complementarity" is very relevant here: two contrasted theories may be able to explain a set of phenomena, while each separately only accounts for some aspects. For full understanding of humanity both the individualistic and the collective-species perspectives are essential. And for discourse on the future of humanity the species perspective is more important, though the individualistic one has to be kept in mind constantly.

24.3 Often there is a real tension between putting human individuals at the center of concern and concentrating on the human species. But there is no strong contradiction. Only individuals exist as visible and concrete entities and have consciousness, feelings, and pondering minds. Therefore, ultimately at stake is the future of living and to be born individuals.

24.4 Nevertheless, humanity as a species is an entity which has emergent properties beyond being a simple aggregation of the traits of individuals living at any particular time. As an HSG you have to consider the evolutionary processes of the human species and its alternative futures as-if humanity is a collective entity composed of generations of conscious individuals, whose thriving is ultimately at stake.

24.5 To ponder in terms of human evolution you must know the ideas of evolutionary theory and its problems, as changing following new findings and theoretical innovations. Reading a few reputable books will meet your needs. But I have met far too many political leaders totally ignorant about basic facts. Therefore, it may be useful to recapitulate some of them here: The evolution of life on Earth goes back about

3.8 billion years. The first Hominids, from which our species evolved, appeared about 2.8 million years ago. Anatomically modern humans emerged around 200,000 to 300,000 years ago in Africa and perhaps also the Middle East. With time they settled nearly all the land of Earth, while advancing from a nomadic way of life as hunter-gatherers to sedentary life as farmers, with the overall number of humans increasing most of the time. Cognitively "modern" humans emerged around 50,000 years ago, probably as a "great leap forward" the nature of which is not clear. Human history as we know it began around 5,500 years ago with the invention of writing. Thus *Homo sapiens* is a very young species in terms of the history of life; and the history of modern humanity is just in its infancy and has a long future before it—if not cut short by premature an end of *Homo sapiens*.

24.6 Relevant is a (necessarily speculative) 2017 estimate of the total number of humans who ever lived, which is about 108 billion, compared to around 7.5 billion living in that year. Thus the proportion of living to dead is about 6%, making our generation a small part of the totality of humanity up till now.

24.7 All species are ephemeral. They exist for some time and then disappear, because of changing ecologies, catastrophes, being displaced by "fitter" ones, or presently unknown causes. A few species probably eliminated themselves by exhausting the food on which they depended. But humanity is unique on Earth in being composed of self-conscious, planning and abstractly thinking persons, having the most complex brain of all life on this planet till now.

24.8 Uniquely so, at least in our Solar System, humanity developed science and technology and very recently acquired the power to eliminate itself by errors and also on purpose. But humanity may also be able to extend its existence till the Cosmos, according to present physics (which may change), becomes inhabitable in about 10^{40} (10 followed by 40 zeroes) years—which is infinitely beyond the time horizon of even the most "futuristic" speculative thinker.

24.9 According to the best scientific contemporary understandings and keeping to a this-worldly frame of thinking, the emergence of the human species depended on a chain of accidents. To quote from Peter Ward and Joe Kirschvink, *A New History of Life: The Radical New Discoveries About the Origins and Evolution of Life on Earth* (2015): "if there is any lesson from life's history, it is that chance has been one of the two major players at the game of life ... and chance makes any attempt at prognosticating events and trends in the future history of life a very chancy proposition." And "The accident killing of the dinosaurs and about 75% of all species about 65 million years ago by the impact of a large asteroid hitting earth and its various aftereffects" enabled mammals to develop, leading with time to the emergence of the human species. The authors add a warning about possible future Permian-like mass extinction as "a prospect far more probable than our species seems to realize."

24.10 This leads to the question if and how far humanity can and should do what no other species on earth could ever consider, namely deliberately influence main features of its future evolution. If we could be sure that "natural" evolutionary processes can be relied upon to unfold in ways conductive to long-term human thriving, deliberate interventions with them, as increasingly feasible, may be dangerous by perhaps ruining favorable evolutionary unfolding. But if ongoing and foreseeable processes can endanger the future of humanity, then seeking ways to redirect them is imperative.

24.11 As matters evolve now, it seems that ongoing human processes will very likely endanger our future as a species. We cannot be sure about the validity of this assessment, but it seems solid enough to serve as a working assumption till a predominance of evidence and pondering proves it wrong. Therefore a deliberate active stance towards evolutionary processes is required, all the more so as spontaneous interventions with evolutionary processes, such as by human enhancement and advancement of general artificial intelligence, pose serious risks unless carefully regulated and rationed.

24.12 The issue is even more complex and also very enigmatic. We understand evolutionary processes only partly and are likely to be wrong about some of them. For instance, there may be some kind of deeper processes built into evolution which drive toward emergence of increasingly complex and "higher level" entities. If so, precreation of Homo superior or building of super-intelligent machines may be the evolutionary fixed destiny of humanity, even at the cost of *Homo sapiens* being displaced and then eliminated.

24.13 All the more so, being able to ponder in terms of the dynamics of human species evolution is critical for the deepest levels of your very being an HSG and makes you very different from nearly all contemporary political leaders and the vast majority of presently living humans. Therefore, you have to invest efforts in constantly upgrading your understanding of evolutionary processes and their possible impacts on the human species. But you cannot jump over the limits of human understanding, nor eliminate the role of chance in evolution. Therefore, decisions trying to influence the future evolution of humanity are by their very nature "fuzzy gambles for fateful stakes." This is an already mentioned critical and also tragic insight, to be discussed soon.

25. RADICALISM

25.1 The Anthroporegenesis epoch is characterized by revolutionary transformations. Therefore, usual patterns of governing, with a lot of procrastination, "more of the same," "it will take care of itself," reliance on legislation to magically impact on reality, and incremental improvements with only few innovative initiatives, will not work. Instead, coping with the challenges posed by the new epoch requires a critical mass of radically novel measures, as illustrated by the proposed humanity-craft principles.

25.2 This involves seeking creative ideas and, after screening, adopting the more promising ones. To do so you have to spend time with creative persons, read a lot, and have on your staff some creative advisors even if their behavior is idiosyncratic. Also, as already suggested, you should facilitate relevant research and humanity-craft think tanks, and maintain close contact with them.

25.3 Such required behavior on your part depends on you yourself being radical, in the sense of seeking cognitively and liking emotionally fargoing changes in major aspects of human life and institutions, but selectively so. Much that is radically new is lousy; and much that has persisted for long continues to be very valuable. Also a lot of continuity, even if non-linear and with swerves into new directions, is essential for social and personal stability.

25.4 This necessitates a quality in your mind that is "rational," in the sense of explicitly recognizing the need for deep changes. But this quality also has to be emotional, seeking and being driven to "compose differently," comparable to an artist founding, or at least rapidly joining a new school of painting. Being "avant-gardist" also expresses what you need emotionally, but tempered by cold thinking on what is really necessary and perhaps possible and, as noted, a sense for the need of a lot of continuity.

25.5 To put it differently, what is needed in your mind, and reflected in your humanity-craft, is "selective radicalism:" changing, even in a revolutionary manner, some aspects of humanity and its institutions, while leaving many others as they are to unfold naturally.

26. CLINICAL PAIN-FEELING CONCERN

26.1 "Clinical concern" as a required core quality includes four integrated components: (1) being "cold," also in the heat of exploding events; (2) readiness to "cut" when necessary, with steady fingers and clear thinking, also when you see, smell, and have blood on your hands; (3) being professional, acting on the basis of the best available knowledge as changing with time, while also rapidly learning from experience; and (4) doing your very best, but not letting identification with the "patient" and human suffering override your pondering and hindering what needs doing.

26.2 But to prevent you from becoming a monster, you must feel the pain of humans. As put by Chaim Potok in his book *The Chosen* (1987):

> "... it is important to know of pain ... It destroys our self-pride, our arrogance, our indifference toward others ... of all people a tsaddik especially must know of pain. A tsaddik must know how to suffer for his people ... He must take their pain from them and carry it on his own shoulders. He must

carry it always. He must grow old before his years. He must cry, in his heart he must always cry. Even when he dances and sings, he must cry for the sufferings of his people."

26.3 Substituting the words "HSG" for "tsaddik" (a Hebrew term meaning "religious sage") and "humanity" for "his people," this passage presents an essential quality of your mind which balances "clinical concern". Only an HSG feeling the pain which she causes in fulfilling his Promethean mission can think and act as a surgeon doing her job without corrupting his conscience.

26.4 This is all the more essential because of the nature of your choices, including your most fateful ones, as fuzzy gambles that can always go wrong at high costs, as discussed next.

27. Face It! You will Be a Fuzzy Gambler for High Stakes

27.1 The simple, exciting, challenging, but very bitter truth that you are a fuzzy gambler for high stakes should not only be at the center of your being and Weltanschauung as an HSG. It is the morally, cognitively and emotionally heaviest burden of being an HSG. You must be fully aware of it and cope with the pains of fuzzy gambling by developing a lot of fuzzy humanity-craft gambling sophistication, both rational and emotional, conscious as well as tacit. A first step in this direction is to understand deep uncertainty, which makes choices into fuzzy gambles.

27.2 The idea of causality, as strongly imprinted by evolution on human minds, is adequate for "common sense," most of practical reasoning, and nearly all natural sciences. But it is inadequate for the complex tasks of political leaders. This was fully recognized by Thucydides, Machiavelli, Bismarck, and many additional insightful decision makers and occasionally admitted by them.

27.3 But none of them ever stood up in public and declared "now, after much pondering, I decided to make the following fuzzy gamble with your future at stake." Humans, despite increasing formal learning, are far from being mature and enlightened enough to swallow this bitter truth. You too must be very careful with your words.

27.4 Awareness of the large role of Fortuna in human affairs resulted all too often in ruinous coping efforts by rulers, such as trusting astrology, soothsayers, oracles etc. Even more dangerous is primitive belief in some kind of "magic," which is expected to influence events. Similarly fatal can be simplistic religious thought. Phillip II, King of Spain, a devout Catholic, led in 1588 an armada against Protestant England. He was warned about bad weather, but was sure that Christ will not let a Holy War fail. The end is known. Do not follow his example! All forms of superstition, astrology, primitive Volk-beliefs etc. are taboo for you! If you have the habit of knocking on wood "for good luck," kick yourself and stop it. And do not tolerate such nonsense by your advisors.

27.5 You have to show confidence in what you decide, in order to mobilize support, prevent useless anxiety, and perhaps achieve a "self-fulfilling prophecy" effect. But in your mind you must be fully and constantly aware of the crucial importance of contingency (in the sense of "it can turn out otherwise"), indeterminacy, random effects, or however it may be called. And you need good familiarity with principles for coping with it.

27.6 First of all, you require an appropriate concept package for thinking on and in terms of deep uncertainty, all the more so as the usual probability scales are misleading when applied to main humanity issues. I propose to you instead a more sophisticated concept package, based in part on what is called "modal logic" but going beyond it.

27.7 The most important distinction is between quantitative and deep uncertainty. Quantitative uncertainty prevails when alternative states of the future are more or less known, but not the likelihood of their realization. Deep uncertainty refers to ignorance about the very shapes of alternative futures. For example, the effects of imposing the death penalty on enemies of humanity are in part known qualitatively, thanks to the logic of classification which can be used here: it may reduce the activities of enemies of humanity, not have any impact on their likelihood, or provoke escalation, in various mixes. But the likelihood of such results is in a state of quantitative uncertainty, which can sometimes be reduced to probabilities or some other scale.

27.8 However, the social results of soft enhancement, such as prolonging life expectancy to 150 high-quality years, are largely in a state of qualitative "deep" uncertainty. Some of them can be guessed, guesstimated, or even estimated. But surprise consequences and also inconceivable ones are nearly certain, producing a state of deep uncertainty.

27.9 When you know very little about possible results of a choice, the decisions you make are "arbitrary" and the issue of the likelihood of different results does not arise. But, in the vast majority of cases, we think (or fool ourselves) that we have some notion of at least a few of the possible results, or that parts of their range is logically or linguistically predetermined. To take an extreme example, what should humanity do if a spaceship from outer space is approaching Earth?

This depends, first of all, on anticipation of its intentions: does it come in order to annihilate our planet or are its intensions peaceful as we understand that term? Thus, even if we are in total ignorance, possible results of letting the spaceship approach Earth are known on the scale of "hostile acts, yes or no." This is good enough for making a choice of yes/no destroying it before reaching Earth.

27.10 Logically, inherent limits of what can happen often enable us to specify some possible results and thus escape total deep uncertainty, though this is up to the quality of our minds: in the case of the alien spaceship, we may or may not consider a third possibility, namely that its commander has not yet decided whether to attack Earth or try to establish friendly relations, having instead the intention to study Earth and its inhabitants before acting one way or another—with his choice depending a lot on how we receive the spaceship. But his reactions too are uncertain: if we received the ship peacefully, he may think Earth is weak and attack it, or in turn open peaceful dialog; but if we attack, he may destroy Earth or view humanity as powerful and demonstrate a will for peaceful cooperation.

27.11 Interaction chains aggravate deep uncertainty: harsher measures against enemies of humanity may cause them to desist, or push them into escalation to the extremes. Coping with such complex and unpredictable interactive processes will stress your mind maximally. Just imagine you have to decide about approaching an alien space ship! The choices you will have to make as an HSG are largely less fatal, but they often are even more complex and some of them are fatal. Definitely all of them which matter are extremely demanding, emotionally as well as cognitively.

27.12 Given some anticipation of the shape of alternative futures, as is usually the case whether correctly so or not, a scale, or at least concept package, for expressing their likelihood is needed. Modal logic, with some variations, distinguishes between impossible, possible, somewhat likely, likely, very likely, certain. To these I add unknown, unknown and unknowable, surprise prone, and unconceivable.

27.13 Recognition of the prevalence, in the epoch of Anthroporegenesis, of much deep as well as quantitative uncertainty concerning the consequences of your main humanity-craft choices logically leads to a conclusion which is profound, very troubling, but inescapable: **Your main decision are fuzzy gambles, in part more bounded and in part more "wild," for high stakes—up to fateful choices with the long-term existence of the human species at stake.**

27.14 Please ponder the following statement: "The processes of history are shaped by a dynamic mix between necessity, chance, and human choice—being altogether contingent." Understanding it is absolutely essential for your Promethean mission, which can now be reformulated as follows: **The essence of the Promethean mission of HSGs consists of high-quality interventions with historic processes with a critical mass adequate for maximally reducing the likelihood of elimination of humanity, preventing catastrophes and lessening Hell on Earth, while significantly increasing the likelihood of long-term thriving of humankind as future generations may wish. But all such interventions are unavoidably "fuzzy gambles," sometimes "wildly" so and sometimes quite bounded, for high and sometimes fateful stakes. Therefore "fuzzy gambling sophistication" is a decisive quality of the mind of an HSG.**

27.15 This very troubling but true understanding brings us to the difficult subject of upgrading the success likelihood of your fuzzy gambles.

But, before proceeding, I invite you to test your understanding of what has been said and the extent to which you have absorbed it in your mind, with the help of a short exercise: A common statement runs as follows: **Level of risk = probability x impact**. Please think it over and explain why it is wrong and indeed very misleading when applied to main risks faced by humanity.

27.16 If you were a participant in one of the workshops I used to give to high-level decision makers, you would now have 30 minutes to formulate your answer, to be later discussed by the group. But you are reading my book, so please stop for as long as it takes you to formulate an answer in your mind, or on your computer. Then compare it with my explanation. In short: Probabilities presume a high degree of knowledge on the likelihood of an event. But there is no basis for anticipating on an exact scale the likelihood of main risks to humanity. As a maximum, one can guesstimate and perhaps estimate the occurrence of catastrophes in the less presumptuous terminology proposed above, such as "likely," adding to the level of confidence of such a statement by explicating that "this is our guesstimate, based on so and so (such as historic precedents). To take a relatively simple example which has been studied, the likelihood of a nuclear full-scale war between India and Pakistan is estimated as "very unlikely, but not impossible." This is a far cry from allocating probabilities with their illusion of exactness, but much nearer to the truth. If to proceed to a more diffuse threat, such as a doomsday sect producing and using a mass-killing virus, the most that can be said with justification is "possible, but with unknowable likelihood."

27.17 To proceed to impacts, uncertainty is even deeper. To return to a possible Indian-Pakistani nuclear war, studies estimate impacts as ranging between some millions of people killed to the worst case of much of the world's ozone layer being destroyed and a "nuclear winter" crippling the monsoons and agriculture worldwide. This is good enough for prudent humanity craft which should take extreme measures to prevent such a war which may have serious global consequences, though this is one estimate among many. Concerning the impacts of, say, intelligent robots, for sure labor markets will implode and much more important consequences are certain, but their range and significance is a matter for speculations and guessing; and they are sure to include what at present is inconceivable. Ergo, **the formula level of risk = probability x impact,** however useful for relatively stable processes and repetitive events susceptible to statistical analysis or fitting reliable quantitative models, **must not be applied to global unprecedented domains which are in a state of deep uncertainty.**

27.18 How to try and improve your fuzzy gambling choices despite the difficulties of doing so is a matter for professionals who should mentor and advise you. But you have to know and understand some main approaches. These include, among others:

(1) When considering options, always think on them both optimistically and pessimistically, but not too extremely so. Then reflect how you will act if the pessimistic anticipations will prove correct.

(2) Often you should follow the principle of prudence, also known as the precautionary principle. This implies preferring lower risks to the chancs of higher gains, especially if failure involves catastrophes. But this is a matter for cost-benefit-risk thinking (not quantitative analysis!). There are cases when some daring is needed, but nearly never when the existence of humanity is likely to be at stake.

(3) There are options which promise very high benefits with a minute danger to the existence of humanity. This, as mentioned, is the case with some high-energy experiments. What to decide depends on values concerning risks, not "rational analysis." The question thus becomes "whose values should shape the choices, as long as there is no legitimate global authority in charge of them?" I invite readers to think about this quandary—I have no ready answer to offer.

(4) Majority opinions should shape democratic decisions, but not outlooks into the future. If an outlook is supported by most of those whom you consult and a different one is presented by a loner, the loner's anticipation has the same (unknown and probably unknowable, and thus a known unknown) likelihood of being correct than that of the majority. (I restrain myself from suggesting that the loner is more likely to be right as he is not infected by groupthink).

(5) Often serious threats to human welfare are of low likelihood and very expensive to prevent. As resources are always scarce, the general tendency is to exclude them from consideration, as their likelihood is below a psychological threshold of being worthy of attention. This is a grave error which you should avoid. But what to do about such dilemmas after a lot of high-quality pondering is far from clear. Much depends on their nature, the resources at your disposal, and your values concerning risk (so-called "lottery values). Still, I tend to recommend giving very high priority to preventing "the nearly worst," even if its likelihood is very low (or unknown—these two modalities must not be mixed up, despite a fallacious psychological tendency to read unknown likeli-

hood as if equivalent to very low likelihood).

(6) Your achievements and failures depend a lot on "luck." You may choose the best option and the results will be dismal. And you may make a stupid decision and results may be heroic. When fuzzy gambles are rather unique (and therefore do not add up to homogenous series justifying statistical evaluation) then the proverb "the proof of the pudding is in the eating," or the prevailing "judgment by results" habits, are invalid and also rather stupid.

27.19 Whatever is said and done, unavoidably engaging in a lot of high-stake fuzzy gambling is a burden that goes along with being an HSG. Consider carefully if you want to carry this heavy mental load before making your existential choice whether to try and become an HSG, or to look for another meaningful life path not imposing such a burden on you.

28. IF YOU FEEL CALLED, DARE THE LEAP!

28.1 Having read and perhaps reread this Memo and, if you wish, engaged in some additional pertinent reading, you are more or less ready to face the existential choice whether to try and become an HSG, at least partly so. In making your decision, the following considerations, among others, should carry much weight:

(1) As emphasized, being an HSG is a matter of degrees. Even a little is a lot, though always more is needed. However, to pass the minimal threshold you must accept and love

"saving humanity from itself" as your main life mission, even if devoting to it only a part of yourself.

(2) You have to invest much into remaking yourself in order to acquire and develop the essential qualities of an HSG. Main options for doing so include a lot of readings, graduate university studies, spending time living and working in countries with a different culture than your homeland, trying to fulfill for some time a position in one of the global governance agencies, having mentors, and gaining a lot of experience dealing with the issues facing humanity.

(3) Despite all qualifications, you may fail in efforts to achieve a leadership position enabling you to act as an HSG. Persistent efforts will increase your chances, but you may still crash without any fault on your part. Accepting stoically your bad luck and seeking another fulfilling life is the best medicine, even if leaving for some time a bitter taste in your mind.

(4) In the best of cases, becoming and being an HSG is very arduous. And your family has to pay the price of your overriding commitment to your Promethean mission, however painful this may be for you and them.

(5) In the vast majority of cases an HSG acts in the political arena. You will have to swallow a lot of shit, be exposed to many corrupting temptations, and unavoidable dirty your hands a lot. At the same time you must keep your inner citadel well protected so as to preserve your character and qualities as an HSG. If this is too much for you, better find another path through life.

(6) However, being an HSG provides you with extraordinary self-realization opportunities. Your mission is intrinsically exciting, exhilarating, and nearly "sacred."

(7) Never mind what others may think about you and future historians will write about you—when your time of death comes, you should be tranquil, knowing that you did your very best for an outstanding purpose.

28.2 Take into account that given the present world order you have no real answer to the question Quo Warranto, which is a legal term requiring a person to show by what warrant an office or franchise is held, claimed, or exercised. It raises the vexing question what legitimizes you as an HSG to presume to take care of the future of humanity without being appointed or authorized by any legitimate body to do so.

28.3 If you are a leader in the United Nations system, you have a partial answer, but this is true only of a minority of HSGs. The genuine answer which I suggest is based on the moral and also widely accepted legal principle of "dire necessity" combined with the moral principle to help those in need even without being asked to do so. Humanity stands in dire need to be saved from itself. Ergo, all who can help doing so are not only permitted to act but morally obliged to do so.

28.4 The validity of this "solution" is strengthened by the already made point that no-one can be authorized by the future to take care of the future. Therefore, your virtues are the best justification for your being an HSG, in addition to dire necessity.

28.5 But a deep problem remains: your intentionality serves as a surrogate for non-existing *Homo sapiens* intentionality. Even if and when the part of humanity living at any given time somehow expresses a collective intentionality, not only is its quality far from assured, but it cannot reflect the intentionality of future generations. Still, it seems reasonable for you to act as-if survival of the human species, which means existence of future generations, is built as an imperative and striving into its very nature as a species, unless decided otherwise by a future generation.

28.6 However obtuse such philosophic meditations may seem to you, paradoxically they strengthen the case for HSGs acting on behalf of humankind: HSGs do not usurp the right of any other entity, because no entity entitled to speak on behalf of the human species as extending over time, including future generations, can exist; and anyone claiming to act "on behalf of humanity" (as distinct from "for humanity") is an imposter. There is no argument giving a living generation the right to make decisions impacting on the fate of future generations, other than dire necessity. All the more so all such decisions must be made by highly responsible and fully qualified agents as-if on behalf and for the human species—as HSGs are supposed to be and do.

28.7 For you as a living person all these considerations are but inputs into your existential choice as an act of will. **What you really need for choosing to try and become an HSG, after understanding what is involved and having reasons to hope that you can acquire the required qualities, is a fire burning in your soul to take up the challenges of saving humanity from itself as an HSG.**

* * *

If you embrace becoming an HSG as your existential choice, as your dharma, as your assigned place in the world, and if you are willing to

toil and sweat and also shed your blood to fulfill your Promethean mission without expecting any extrinsic reward—then this "Mirror for Rulers" is respectfully dedicated to you!

Recommended Readings

To put you in the right mood, I recommend that you spend some time enjoying Terry Virts, *View From Above: An Astronaut Photographs the World* (Washington, DC: National Geographic, 2017), or a similar publication which presents you with your main domain of concern: the Earth on which humanity dwells as seen from space.

The first book to read is the essay by Max Weber, *Politics as a Vocation*, discussed in Section 22.1. Then jump to H.G. Wells, *The World Set Free*, published in 1914. It is quoted in some of the memoranda dealing with the building and use of the first nuclear bombs, because it foresaw a terrible war leading to a world state developing into a utopia.

Then proceed to Richard Rhodes, *The Making of the Atomic Bomb: The 25th Anniversary Edition* (New York: Simon & Schuster, 2012). Dealing with much more than implied by the title, it will introduce you to the issues at the center of this Memo.

A good introduction to the theory of evolution and its development is Niles Eldredge, *Eternal Ephemera: Adaptation and the Origin of Species from the Nineteenth Century through Punctuated Equilibria and Beyond* (New York: Columbia University Press, 2015), which deals a lot with the appearance and disappearance of species, as relevant to the Memo. Then please read the important iconoclastic book by Thomas Nagel, *Mind and Cosmos: Why the Materialist Neo-Darwinian Conception of Nature is Almost Certainly False* (Oxford: Oxford University Press, 2012). Moving on to the human species, recommended are Yuval Noah Harari, *Sapiens: A Brief History of Humankind* (New York:

HarperCollins, 2015); and Peter Ward and Joe Kirschvink, *A New History of Life: The Radical New Discoveries About the Origins and Evolution of Life on Earth* (New York: Bloomsbury, 2015). Striking is Daniel Lord Smail, *On Deep History and the Brain* (Berkeley: University of California Press, 2008).

On risks to humanity the classic book is Sir Martin Rees, *Our Final Hour: A Scientist's Warning: How Terror, Error, and Environmental Disaster Threaten Humankind's Future in this Century—On Earth and Beyond* (New York: Basic Books, 2003). A comprehensive collection of essays covering the ground is Nick Bostrom and Milan M. Ćirkobić, eds., *Global Catastrophic Risks* (Oxford: Oxford University Press, 2008). More concise and up-to-date is the The Global Challenges Foundation Report, *Global Catastrophic Risks 2017* (Stockholm: Global Challenges Foundation, 2017), accessible on https://api.globalchallenges.org/static/files/Global%20Catastrophic%20Risks%202017.pdf.

For detailed studies of the potentials and risks of superintelligence and ways to cope with them I recommend Nick Bostrom, *Superintelligence: Paths, Dangers, Strategies* (Oxford: Oxford University Press, 2014); and Murray Shanahan, *The Technological Singularity* (Cambridge, MA: MIT Press, 2015).

A recommended book presenting in a personal narrative the nature of errors as a main unavoidable risk facing humanity is James Reason, *A Life in Error: From Little Slips to Big Disasters* (Boca Raton, IL: CRC Press, 2013).

For a different approach than mine to the issues facing humanity, read David Rothkopf, *The Great Questions of Tomorrow* (New York: Simon & Schuster, 2017).

An illuminating example of doomsday cults is provided in Robert Jay Lifton, *Destroying the World to Save It: Aum Shinrikyo, Apocalyptic Violence and the New Global Terrorism* (New York: Holt, 2000).

Main issues of human enhancement are covered by the essays in Max More and Natasha Vita-More, eds., *The Transhuman Reader: Classical and Contemporary Essays on the Science, Technology, and Philosophy of the Human Future* (Malden, MA: Wiley-Blackwell, 2013); and Julian Savulescu and Nick Bostrom, eds., *Human Enhancement* (Oxford: Oxford University Press, 2013).

On human extinction the classical book still worth reading is John Leslie, *The End of the World: The Science and Ethics of Human Extinction* (London: Routlede, 1996). A concise up-to-date text on global extinctions is Elizabeth Kolbert, *The Sixth Extinction: An Unnatural History* (New York: Holt, 2015).

For considering the idea of advancing the human species as a collective moral agency, read Michael E. Bratman, *Shared Agency: A Planning Theory of Acting Together* (Oxford: Oxford University Press, 2014); and Deborah Perron Tolleffsen, *Groups as Agents* (Cambridge, UK: Polity, 2015). Demanding but very important is Raimo Tuoela, *Social Ontology: Collective Intentionality and Group Agency* (Oxford: Oxford University Press, 2013).

The thesis that only large scale violence can significantly reduce economic inequality is forcefully presented in Walter Scheidel, *The Great Leveler: Violence and the History of Inequality from the Stone Age to the Twenty-First Century* (Princeton: Princeton University Press, 2017).

A good example of ideas on quality politics influenced by Chinese traditions is Daniel A. Bell, *The China Model: Political Meritocracy and the Limits of Democracy* (Princeton: Princeton University Press, 2015), to be followed by Jason Brennan, *Against Democracy* (Princeton: Princeton University Press, 2016).

On "luck," a good collection of essays is Duncan Pridtchard and Lee John Whittington, eds., *The Philosophy of Luck* (Malden, MA: Wiley Blackwell, 2015).

On some of the ways of pondering fitting humanity-craft composing, read Emiliano Ippoliti, ed., *Heuristic Reasoning* (New York: Springer, 2016), to be supplemented by an introduction to quite different but relevant classical Chinese approaches, namely François Jullien, *A Treatise on Efficacy: Between Western and Chinese Thinking* (Honolulu: University of Hawai'i Press, 2004).

Outstanding on a crucial quality of the mind of an HSG is Pierre Hadot. *The Inner Citadel: The Meditations of Marcus Aurelius* (Cambridge, MA: Harvard University Press, 2001). On existentialism, read Sarah Bakewell, *At the Existentialist Café: Freedom, Being, and Apricot Cocktails* (New York: Other Press, 2016). Relevant virtues are presented in Robert C. Roberts **and** W. Jay Wood, *Intellectual Virtues: An Essay in Regulative Epistemology* (New York: Oxford University Press, 2007).

A concise introduction to the politics of climate change, exhibiting the incapacities of contemporary global institutions to cope with relatively clear issues, is Mark Maslin, *Climate Change: A Very Short Introduction* (Oxford: Oxford University Press, Third Edition, 2014). The hopelessness of relying on prevailing politics to bring about the needed global order is demonstrated by Mark Mazower, *Governing the World: The History of an Idea, 1815 to the Present* (New York: Penguin, 2012).

More relevant than many will admit may be Adrian Goldsworthy, *Pax Romana: War, Peace and Conquest in the Roman World* (New Haven: Yale University Press, 2016).

Other approaches to global order than mine are well represented by David Held, *Cosmopolitanism: Ideals and Realities* (Cambridge, UK: Polity, 2010); and the already classic book by Henry Kissinger, *World Order: Reflections on the Character of Nations and the Course of History* (New York: Penguin, 2014).

For articles relevant to an HSG, see the journals *Futures, World Futures Review* and *Global Policy,* which you should check regularly.

For an enlightening biography of a proto-HSG read Roger Lipsey, *Hammarskjöld: A Life* (Ann Arbor: University of Michigan Press, 2013).

A model of what a global humanity-craft think tank is needed for is provided by Andrew R, Hoehn et al., *Strategic Choices for a Turbulent World: In Pursuit of Security and Opportunity* (Santa Monica, CA: RAND Corporation, 2017), accessible on http://www.rand.org/content/dam/rand/pubs/research_reports/RR1600/RR1631/RAND_RR1631.pdf.

A good example of "first aid" proposals which can help bridge ruptures for some time, see Graeme Maxton and Jorgen Randers, *Reinventing Prosperity: Managing Economic Growth to Reduce Unemployment, Inequality and Climate Change* (Vancouver: Graystone Books, 2016).

To return to political leadership, after Weber worth reading on leadership in general is Shalom Saada Saar, with Michael J. Hargrove,

Leading with Conviction: Mastering the Nine Critical Pillars of Integrated Leadership (San Francisco: Jossey-Bass, 2013). Useful on political leadership are Michael Foley, *Political Leadership: Themes, Contexts, and Critilques* (Oxford: Oxford University Press, 2013), together with Paul t'Hart, *Understanding Public Leadership* (New York: Palgrave, 2014), to be contrasted with my own much more radical views in Yehezkel Dror, *Avant-Garde Politician: Leaders for a New Epoch* (Washington, DC: Westphalia Press, Imprint of Policy Studies Organization, 2014).

There are many movies, novels and books depicting Apocalypse. The one I like best is Walter M. Miller, Jr., *A Canticle for Leibowitz* (New York: EOS, 2006 [1959]). The seven volumes of the *Foundation* series by Isaac Asimov stimulated my life-long interest in "rise and decline," leading me with time to human evolution and the future of the human species, with this book being one of the results. Therefore it is only fair that I recommend it to you for stimulating pleasure reading, together with the stimulating book by Russell Blackford, *Science Fiction and the Moral Imagination: Visions, Minds, Ethics* (New York: Springer, 2017).

Nearly all movies and TV series dealing with rulers, such as West Wing, House of Cards, and so on, may be good for leisure, but are totally misleading on realities and fail to present any stimulating ideas. The one distinguished exception which I strongly recommend is the 2016 HBO series *The Young Pope*. In addition to being very creative, in parts it well presents the difficulties of a "different" ruler confronting traditional ones.

Acknowledgements

I am most grateful to the president of the Policy Studies Organization (PSO), Professor Paul Rich, and especially to its director, Daniel Gutierrez-Sandoval, for undertaking publication of this book. Having been associated for many years with PSO adds to my delight at having this additional opportunity to cooperate in a joint venture.

I am also indebted to the designer Jeffrey Barnes for a highly professional job.

And a special "thank you" is due to Puder PR, its President and Founder Arik Puder and all it's highly professional staff for help in getting this book to the intended audiences.

Last, but far from least, I am very grateful to Professor Jim Dator for important revision suggestions; to Dr. Michal Marien for pertinent comments; and to my niece, Ayelet Dekel, Founder & Editor, Midnight East (www.midnighteast.com), for applying her literary skills to the text.

Made in the USA
Middletown, DE
25 July 2018